HIND

A PRIMER

Rational Exploration of The World's Oldest Religion

Dr. Raghavendra S. Prasad
MD, FAAFP, FACIP, CMD, WCC

First Published in 2012
Hinduism A Primer
Dr. Raghavendra S. Prasad
© Author

Price US :$10

ISBN 979-1-4675-4343-9

Library of Congress Control Number (LCCN): 201291457

Publisher:
Kalyani Raghavam Publications
1320 N. Cedar Hill Road
Cedar Hill, Texas 75104
USA

Processing and printed at: Pragati Offset Pvt. Ltd., Hyderabad, India

DEDICATION

Dedicated to my father,
Sudanagunta Kotaiah Chowdary
my first Guru who sowed the seed of
spirituality in my heart at a tender age.

Dedicated to my dear wife,
Kalyāni
(a true Saha Dharma Chārini),
who travelled with me as a friend in my journey of
spirituality giving me support and practical advice,
that helped me turn into a better human being.

Humbly dedicated
at the lotus feet of my most beloved Guru
Bhagawān Sri Sathya Sāi Bāba
who is responsible for the insight through which
I could explore spirituality in a new light.

TABLE OF CONTENTS

LIST OF PHOTOS AND DIAGRAMS

1. OM – Radiating Energies
2. River
3. Modes of transportation-on foot
4. Modes of Transportation-by bus
5. Modes of Transportation-by airplane
6. Modes of Transportation-by ship
7. Devotional singing
8. Service activities-Playing with the Blind
9. Service activities-Feeding the poor
10. Service activities-Medical Service
11. Service activities-Medical Service
12. Reading spiritual books
13. Meditation
14. Chakrās
15. Madhwāchārya
16. Ramānujāchārya
17. Sankarāchārya
18. Hindu worship ritual
19. Ten Avatārās of Vishnu (Dasāvatār)
20. Dasāvatārs
21. Brahma (Creator)
22. Vishnu (Protector)
23. Maheswara (Destroyer)
24. Dakshināmurty
25. Dattātreya
26. Veda Vyāsa

27. Ādi Sankarāchārya
28. Dr. Prasad with Sathya Sai Bābā
29. Vegetarian food
30. Sacred cows
31. Cow and Calf
32. Saivism
33. Vaishnavism
34. Saktism
35. Jainism-Mahāvir
36. Jainism-Five Mahāvratās
37. Buddhism-Sāranāth Stupa
38. Buddhism- Celebration
39. Sikhism-Golden Temple
40. Sikhism-Musicians
41. Hindu Marriage-Fire Offering
42. Hindu Marriage-Pouring Saffron Rice
43. Hindu Marriage-Blessings from Parents
44. Hindu Funeral-Body being carried to Cremation Ground
45. Hindu Funeral-Manikarnika Ghat, Vāranāsi
46. OM Symbol
47. Sacred Dot (Bindi)
48. Red Tilaka Powder in Market
49. Sacred Ash (Vibhuti)
50. Siva Lingam in Vāranāsi Temple
51. Siva Lingam in Madhurai Temple
52. Lakshmi
53. Saraswati
54. Durga
55. Nataraja
56. Vishnu
57. Ganesa
58. Prārabdha Karma

Hinduism is the world's oldest religion. It is based on Vedic knowledge. True exploration of this ancient religion should be done with Vedic vision – 'the inner vision'. My years of spiritual quest through the Ramakrishna Math and Mission and Chinmaya Mission, finally landed me at the lotus feet of my spiritual preceptor (Guru), Bhagawan Sri Sathya Sāi Bāba. It is IIe who opencd me to a renewed vision of spirituality in general and Hinduism in particular.

While there are many books on the subject, I tried to share with the readers the deeper insights that I experienced through my personal spiritual quest. I tried to be candid in unfolding the truths about several topics discussed in this book.

I sincerely hope that this will serve the needs of both the novice (as a primer) and the seasoned (as a new perspective).

ACKNOWLEDGEMENTS

My most humble salutations at the lotus feet of my beloved Guru Bhagavan Sri. Sathya Sāi Bāba for inspiring me to the task and for using me as a fitting instrument in bringing out this 'Hinduism-A Primer'

Any worthwhile task is a result of contribution of large number of people. I am blessed to have friends who considered this project as one of their own and gave me help in any area of my need. While it only took few weeks for writing the content, it took countless hours for four months for the pre publication work of the manuscript.

Particularly the effort was amplified because of simultaneous publishing of both English and Telugu versions. I would like to take this opportunity to thank number of people who shared their time, effort and skills to help me in this project.

I want to thank my good friend Sri. Maddali Raghuram of Kinnera Art Theaters. He worked tirelessly in managing the publication in India. His effort is particularly heartening since he did this in spite his surgery, hospital stay and rehabilitation in between.

I would like to thank Sri. Mylavarapu Srinivasa Rao for doing an excellent job in translating the English manuscript into Telugu,

I want to thank Sri. A.S. Murthy for editing the manuscript, Sri. Suryachandra Reddy of Himalayan Graphics for guidance, Smt. Bommiraju Lakshmi for Telugu DTP work, Bali and Prem Manda for cover design, Srinivas Danda and Sateesh Mamillapalli for general help with computer and my dear wife who spent innumerable hours reading and editing the manuscript along with me. In conclusion I would like to thank Pragati Offset Printers for excellence in printing. All your contributions are greatly appreciated and cherished.

– Your Raghavendra Prasad.

The present most outstanding need is for the availability of direct and straightforward explanations of the Vedic knowledge, called Hinduism by many. This is especially in the form of books for the Indian youth who should have a more thorough understanding of how profound their culture is, and for others who are looking for deeper levels of spiritual knowledge. In this way, they need to have sources of knowledge that can show that Hinduism is not as complicated as some people seem to propose, and that through a simple but full presentation they can see how much it has to offer, and how they can participate in it. Plus, they have to see what benefits they can derive from it.

The advantage of the Vedic spiritual process is that it is a means by which those who practice it can become elevated to the position in which they can have their own spiritual perceptions. This is actually expected of those on the Vedic path. It is not based on blind faith, even though everyone starts with faith. But after serious practice, one can begin to have his or her own direct realizations. That is the difference between faith and deeper realizations, which is much farther than a mere belief system, or a dogma that must be accepted whether it is fully understood or realized or not.

I have had much appreciation of the writings I have done through this same process of explaining the Vedic tradition in a simple and straightforward manner, based on both Sāstric knowledge and personal realizations, but we need more books like that to help saturate the marketplace. We need to have more books that can guide a person along this path that can show that it is not complicated, but actually quite easy and joyful. As it is described by Lord Krishna in the Bhagavad Gita: "This knowledge is the king of education, the most secret of all secrets. It is the purest knowledge, and because it gives direct perception of the self by realization, it is the perfection of religion. It is everlasting, and it is joyfully performed." (Bg. 9.2)

Therefore, I am glad to see this book by Dr. Raghavendra S. Prasad that easily and quickly takes the reader through the basic knowledge of the Vedic tradition, Hinduism, and brings the reader to a deeper level of understanding what this process can offer them.

Hare Krishna,

Stephen Knapp (Sri Nandanandana dasa), author of over 20 books on Vedic culture.

www.stephen-knapp.com

HIS HOLINESS
BHAGAWAN SRI SRI SRI
VISWAYOGI VISWAMJEE MAHARAJ
VISWAMANDIRAM
Krishna Nagar, Guntur
AP, India
www.Viswaguru.com

Dr. Raghavendra Prasad's "Hinduism – A primer" is a must for anyone desiring to know about Sanātana Dharma and the rich Vedic tradition. The author is to be commended for covering such a wide range of topics and in such a slim volume - a real achievement in itself. If we consider that there are a number of photographs and illustrations it goes to show how the author has very skillfully conveyed the essential meaning using a combination of picture and text.

Many "primers" exist on the topic of Hinduism but few have achieved the sweeping coverage of this offering. Its appeal lies in the simplicity with which complex topics are rendered easily intelligible without losing the reader in mere dialectics. On the one hand we have simple topics, such as, what each festival is about to the abstruse, such as, the Vedic Mahāvākyās. The sheer range of topics and their coverage is enlightening. It is not a mere scholarly account but rather a recounting of the insights that the author has gained as a result of his spiritual sadhana. Every topic is explored with respect to its outer reason or purpose as also its inner or spiritual purpose. The decline of a religion or a way of life is when the outer ritual is emphasized without clarifying the inner purpose or goal of the ritual. This book goes a long way in helping dispel such ignorance. Those who are familiar with Hinduism or Sanātana Dharma too will find many golden nuggets of wisdom which are also very practical in their scope.

The author while acknowledging his Guru – Bhagawan Sri Sathya Sāi Bāba – also shows due respect and reverence to other gurus as well. This is a true measure of his maturity and understanding; it is also a reflection of Sanātana Dharma which welcomes every path as long as that path fosters the goal of unity and takes you closer to the ultimate goal of recognizing one's own latent divinity.

Dr. Raghavendra Prasad is a very disciplined and sincere spiritual seeker. I whole heartedly congratulate and bless him and his family for this contribution to all the seekers of Sanātana Dharma.

Divine Blessings

SRI SRI SRI VISWAYOGI VISWAMJEE MAHARAJ

DIVINE BLESSINGS

Satguru Sri Paripurnānanda Giri Swamy

It gives me great pleasure to write a few words about the treatise authored by Dr. Raghavendra S. Prasad, whom I've known for many years, during his spiritual journey in Hinduism as well as his interest in India's rich tradition and culture.

As I went through the manuscript, I was impressed by its simplicity and clarity. I find the rendering just superb and marvelous. The seed sprouts out from earth and grows up to be a tree offering its fruits to all. Similarly Dr. Prasad brought out his thoughts about Hinduism from his spiritual heart. His good samskaras inherited from fore fathers, intense spiritual sadhana, blessings from his guru combined with his direct experience of knowledge as revelation was seen clearly in this book.

Dr. Prasad has drawn upon his experiences and broad knowledge of Hinduism to produce a comprehensive primer which distills the essence of the world's oldest religion. This book is a trove of information for anyone wishing to understand the basic tenets of Sanātana Dharma. This book is a must book to have in home and public libraries. I pray the almighty and Parama Guru Sri Malayalaswami to bestow his endless blessings upon the author and his family.

Satguru Sri Paripurnānanda Giri Swamy
SRI VYASASRAMAM
(Via) Erpedu, Chittoor Dist. A.P – 577621, INDIA

Swami Bodhananda Saraswati

Spiritual Director and Founder of
The Sambodh Center for Human Excellence

"A comprehensive taxonomy of Hindu Dharma Tradition, this slim volume serves the purpose of a teaching note for teachers of Hinduism and as a reference book of salient features of Hinduism for the lay Hindu believers. Dr. Prasad, fusing insights from his personal religious practices, wide reading of Hindu scriptures, association with great Hindu spiritual leaders and discipline of his scientific training, has produced a powerful package of wisdom and knowledge as a gift for the one billion strong global Hindu community."

The Sambodh Society, Inc.
1826 Charter Avenue
Portage, Michigan 49004

1. SANĀTANA DHARMA

Sanātana Dharma is the original name of Hinduism. Sanātana generally means ancient. In the context of Hinduism it means 'eternal'. Dharma means right conduct. Sanātana Dharma means code of right conduct eternally followed from times immemorial. Hence, Hinduism is called the eternal way of right living. Sanātana also means beyond time, good for all times. Dharma also means "Rita". Rita is the rhythms of nature/creation. Cosmic rhythm which is there from times immemorial is Sanātana Dharma.

It is universally applicable religion for all times and all people. This has no known founder. It is based on Vedas that are revelations to the sages. It has no single book, but has a full library of scriptures. The Bhagavad-Gita which is part of Bhishma Parva is considered to be the most revered book of Hindus.

2. ORIGIN OF THE WORD HINDUISM

Persians referred to the people on the banks of river Sindhu as Hindus. They mispronounced "S" for "H". Thus the people in the Indian sub-continent were referred as Hindus. This has later become synonym to the predominant religion Sanātana Dharma practiced in the sub-continent as Hinduism.

3. BELIEFS OF HINDUISM

Hindus believe many diverse things, but the following are a few concepts on which most Hindus concur.

A.   There is one all-pervasive Supreme Being who is both immanent and transcendent, both manifest and un-manifest Reality.

B.   The universe undergoes endless cycles of creation, sustenance and dissolution.

C.   All souls are evolving towards union with God and will ultimately find Moksha through spiritual knowledge and liberation from the cycle of birth and rebirth. Not a single soul is eternally deprived of this destiny.

D.   Karmā is the law of cause and effect, wherein each individual creates his own destiny by his thoughts, words and deeds.

E.   Soul reincarnates evolving through many births until all karmas (Kārmic baggage is burned) are resolved.

F.   Divine beings exist in unseen worlds and that temple worship, rituals, sacraments as well as personal devotionals create a communion with these devas and gods.

G.   A spiritually awakened Master or Sat Guru is essential to guide us to know the Transcendent Absolute, as are personal discipline, good conduct, purification, self enquiry and meditation.

H.   All life is sacred, to be loved and revered, and therefore practice Ahimsa, non-violence.

I. No one particular religion is the only way of salvation above all others. Hinduism believes that all genuine religious paths are facets of God's Pure Love and Light, deserving tolerance and understanding.

J. God is Omniscient, Omnipotent, and Omnipresent. They feel that every speck of creation is permeated by divinity, hence show reverence to each and every thing in creation.

4. UNIQUENESS OF HINDUISM

"If there were to be a single universal religion in the world that would be Vedāntic Hinduism" said Swami Vivekananda. He said this because Hinduism has the characteristics to be called a universal religion. Hinduism –

A. Caters to the needs of people of all levels of understanding and all temperaments.

B. Accepts all religions as different paths to reach the same destination.

C. Considers scriptures only as road maps to facilitate spiritual journey, not as the goal in itself.

D. Believes that all of creation and all creatures animate or inanimate are forms of Divinity (Omnipresent Divinity).

E. Does not believe in religious conversion.

F. Does not have a founder or a book or a time it was started.

> *"I am proud to belong to a religion which has taught the world both tolerance and universal acceptance. We believe not only in universal toleration, but we accept all religions as true. As different streams having different sources all mingle their waters in the sea, so different tendencies, various though they appear, crooked or straight, all lead to God".*
>
> **Swami Vivekananda**

5. GOAL OF LIFE

Goal of life according to Hinduism is to be happy. Un-ending happiness is the goal. This is not the fleeting moments of joy followed by suffering that life presents to all. In order to get this un-ending happiness (Ānanda) we need to get back to our source, home (Paramātman). This is because, our very source (home) is Ānanda.

Our goal is to know who we really are, to know where we have come from. Once we realize this we become one with our source (Brahman). This state of realization of our source is called Moksha, Self Realization, Liberation or Bliss. Our mind will be restless till such time. When one reaches this goal he will be beyond the world of duality (duality is an attitude of separation of the creator and creation) that is responsible for the worldly pain and suffering and he will attain unending happiness (Ānanda).

"We must be bright and cheerful. Long faces do not make religion. Religion should be the most joyful thing in the world, because it is the best"

Swami Vivekananda

6. FOURFOLD PATH

Hinduism offers four different paths to reach the goal of life, depending on the person's innate nature and level of knowledge. One is free to follow one, two or a combination of paths (this is more often the case).

Bhakti   Karma   Jnāna   Rāja

Of these four paths Bhakti is the easiest path in which the equipment needed is readily available to all. This equipment is love. That is why this is compared to traveling on foot. Karma Yoga is compared to travel by bus, Jnāna Yoga is compared to flying by air while Rāja Yoga is compared to sailing by a ship.

For example, to travel from Los Angeles to San Francisco, there are several choices. Those that have no resources can travel on foot (Bhakti), those with limited resource can travel by bus (Karma), those that have more resources can fly (Jnāna) or the ones that are adventurous can go by the boat (Rāja). They also can walk for a while, go by the bus for a while, go by the boat for a while and fly to their destination.

As we travel towards our destination, there are some milestones that we come across to help us understand whether we are on the right course and also to let us know how close we are to the destination. These milestones are peace and joy. When we are on our spiritual path, we should feel more and more peaceful. We should feel more and more joyful. We should feel more and more grateful. We should feel more and more contented. We should feel less and less critical of others. We should start seeing sparks of goodness even in the so called bad people. We should get more and more connected to people around us. We should start enjoying the beauty and harmony that is all around us. We should start experiencing the invisible hand of divinity in each and every thing. We become a happy spectator, an actor in our own life's drama and also enjoy the skill of the director (God), who is directing the whole show.

A.   Path of Devotion (Bhakti Yoga):

This is the path of devotion that is possible for all. Bhakti is intense love for God. Love is the emotion of creation. Through this love one can connect to the very source of creation. Innumerable saints and sages attained Moksha through this path.

Group devotional singing (Bhajans) by Sāi devotees

Nine types of devotion (Nava Vidha Bhakti)

1.	Sravanam:	Listening to the stories and glories of God.
2.	Kirtanam:	Singing the glories of God.
3.	Smaranam:	Reciting the names of God.
4.	Pāda Sevanam:	Serving the feet of God.
5.	Archanam:	Worshipping God.
6.	Vandanam:	Saluting God.
7.	Dāsyam:	Servitude to God.
8.	Sakhyam:	Friendship with God.
9.	Ātma Nivedanam:	Total surrender to God.

Out of the nine types of devotion, Smaranam, also called Nāmasmaranam (reciting the name of God as continuous chanting) is the easiest and is considered the best in these times of Kali Yuga. As we chant the name repeatedly, the form the name represents comes into our mind. The attributes of that form are slowly imbibed by the devotee ("Yad bhāvam tat bhavati" - as you think, so you become). This brings transformation in the devotee to become a better person.

Sixteen steps of Hindu worship (Puja) ritual : (Shodasopachār):

There are Sixteen Upachārās (steps in service to the deity). Most Hindus on daily basis do devotional practices (Puja) in their homes in the designated shrine room (Puja room). After taking bath, they typically do Puja (devotional ritual) by following sixteen steps in full or partially as follows.

1.	Āvāhana:	Welcoming of the deity
2.	Āsanam:	Seating of the deity

3.	Pādyam:	Offering water to wash the feet
4.	Arghyam:	Offering water to wash hands
5.	Āchamanam:	Offering water to sip and rinse
6.	Snānam:	Providing a bath
7.	Vastram:	Offering fresh clothes
8.	Yagnopaveetam:	Offering fresh sacred thread
9.	Gandham:	Offering aromatic sandal paste
10.	Alankāram:	Offering decoration
11.	Pushpam:	Offering of flowers
12.	Dhupam:	Burning incense
13.	Deepam:	Waving lights
14.	Naivedyam:	Offering food
15.	Tāmbulam:	Offering betel leaves, nuts
16.	Karpura Neerājanam:	Ārati & sending off.

However, on weekends, special occasions (like birth days, marriage anniversaries etc.) and on festival days, Hindus go to the temples and offer prayers with devotional services performed by temple priests.

In Hinduism the priests do not preach. They restrict themselves to perform rituals of devotion (Pujās). Sages and saints, who are self-realized souls do the preaching and teaching to the disciples.

Four kinds of devotees (by their nature):

Chaturvidhā bhajante mām janāssukritinorjuna
Artho jijnāsurarthārthee jnānee cha Bharatarshabha". Gita: 7-16

Arjunā!, Four kinds of virtuous persons worship me, the one in troubles, the one who seeks power and wealth, the seeker of knowledge and the seeker of Moksha. Oh the best of the Bharatās.

These are: the one who is in Ārti, Ardhārthi, Jijnāsu and Mokshakāmi. Most often one starts in Ārti and ascends up as Jijnāsu & Mokshakāmi as in the case of Dhruva.

1. Ārti: One who calls upon God when in trouble.

2. Ardhārthi: One who prays for material wealth and power.

3. Jijnasu: Seeker of knowledge.

4. Mokshakāmi: Seeker of self realization.

Out of these four kinds, Ārti and Ardhārthi are the most common type of devotees. However, even these devotees after a while get purified and transform into Jijnāsu and Mokshakāmi.

B.   Path of Selfless Service (Karma Yoga):

This is also called Nishkāma Karma Mārga. Actions done with focus on results in mind, increase the Kārmic baggage of the individual. However selfless service (Nishkāma Karma) done with non-attachment to the fruits of action, brings in purity of heart and sublimation of ego (Chitta Suddhi).

Ego sublimation is the final frontier to overcome in spiritual journey. This ego sublimation is accomplished through selfless action (Nishkama Karma). Upanishads declare

"Na Karmanā Na prajayā na dhanena
Tyāgenaike Amritatwa Mānasuh
*   - (Kaivalyopanishad 3rd Sloka)"*

Dallas Sāi volunteers serving the blind in Light House for the Blind

Dallas Sāi volunteers preparing food for the needy at Family Gateway Center

This means neither through doing deeds, nor through earning money nor even through progeny, does one attain liberation. Only through sacrifice, is immortality achieved. This sacrifice is not material wealth alone but the sacrifice of ego (body mind identification).

All Karmās produce results whether we desire or not. Good Karmās produce good results and bad Karmās produce bad results for the owner of the Karmā. Karmā done without ownership produces no Kārmic baggage, but purifies the heart by burning the ego.

All results good or bad go to one's own personal account created by God, in the bank of divinity. The dividend we reap from this bank is Chitta Suddhi (purity of heart). Through Chitta Suddhi alone true knowledge is revealed to us.

Kārmic baggage and ego are hindrances to self realization. Nishkāma Karma (selfless action) reduces Kārmic baggage and sublimates ego. Thus it makes the spiritual ground fertile so that Jnāna (cosmic knowledge) can germinate, grow and produce the harvest of Moksha.

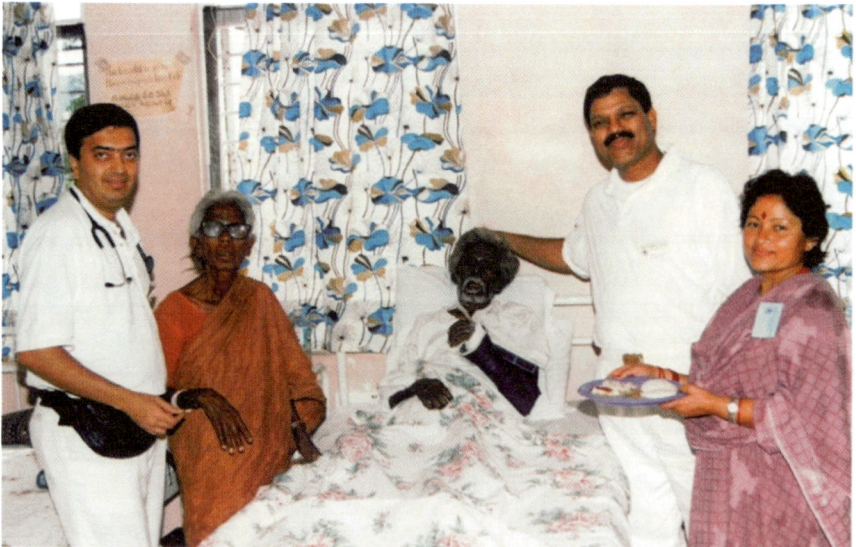

Sāi volunteer doctors service in Medical Camp at Puttaparthy, India

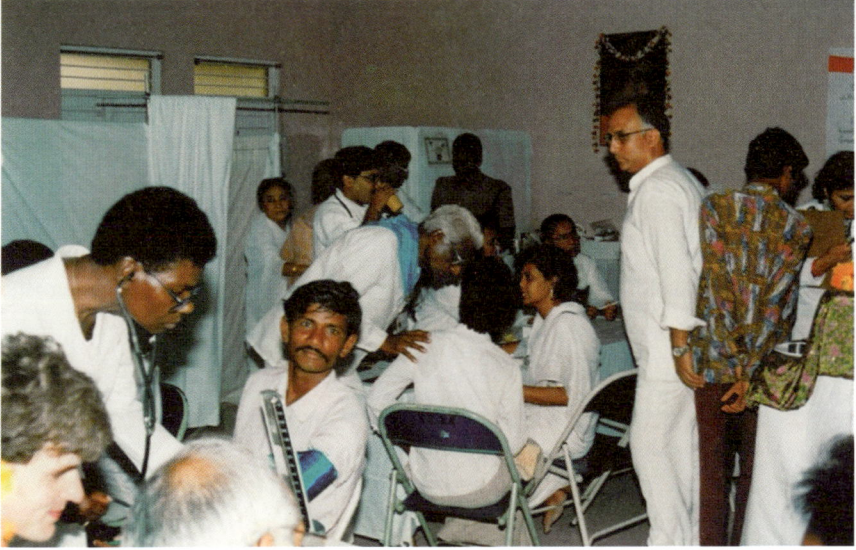
Overseas Sāi volunteers working at Medical Camp at Puttaparthy, India

Three qualities of selfless service (Nishkāma Karma):

1. **Yajna Drishti -**
    "Yagnārdhat Karmanāh" Gita 3-9: meaning work for common good of humanity only.
2. **Non-attachment -**
    without attachment to fruits of action.
3. **Action as service to God -**
    "Yat Karoti - Madarpanam" Gita 9-27: meaning doing work in surrender to God.

Actions done selflessly, without attachment to the fruits of action and done as service to God produce the best results (purity of heart and ego sublimation), without building Kārmic baggage for future lives.

The more we come out and do good to others, the more our hearts will be purified, and God will be in them.

Swami Vivekananda

C.   Path of Knowledge (Jnāna Yoga):

This path is for the ones that are blessed with a discriminating mind who are inquisitive about the goal and purpose of life and living. This kind of seeker will not be satisfied with Bhakti or Karma alone. Sometimes, when a devotee spends some time in devotional practices and selfless service, then one becomes ripe to enquire further and becomes a Jnāna yogi. All the other three Yogās finally culminate in Jnāna yoga.

Upanishads declare "Adwaita Darsanam Jnānam" meaning experience of oneness in creation is knowledge.

Ancient Spiritual Literature

"Brahma Vit Brahmaiva Bhavati" meaning the one who knows Brahman becomes Brahman. "Jnanāgni Dagdha Karmāni" as said in the Gita, means proper knowledge of Brahman shall burn large heaps of Kārmic baggage pent up over several lives. When purity of heart (Chitta Suddhi) is developed through unison of thoughts, words and actions (Trikarana Suddhi) and through selfless service (Nishkāma Karma) by ego sublimation, the all pervading cosmic knowledge comes as revelation (Sruti-Veda).

The following four types of practices help a Jnāna Yogi to get the desired goal of Moksha. These are 1. Discrimination 2. Detachment 3. Serenity, sense control, faith, patience and single pointedness 4. Strong yearning for liberation.

Four practices (Sādhana Chatushtaya):

1. Viveka: - Discrimination (real vs. unreal).

2. Vairāgya: - Detachment from unreal.

3. Shad Sampat :   - Six wealths:
       a. Sama: -serenity of mind
       b. Dama: -control of senses
       c. Uparati: -mind control
       d. Titiksha: -intensity, endurance
       e. Sraddha: -faith
       f. Samadhāna: -single pointedness of mind

4. Mumukshatwam-strong yearning for liberation.

D. Path of Contemplation (Rāja Yoga)

Yoga is defined by sage Patanjali as "Chitta Vritti Nirodhah" - Stilling the wavering mind is Yoga. To achieve this task, sage Patanjali declared Ashtānga Yoga. Āsanās and Prānāyāma constitute a sub-division of Rāja Yoga called Hatha Yoga. Stillness of mind is a must for connecting to the cosmic frequency, though which we can tap into the cosmic knowledge. This Eight-fold path delineated by sage Patanjali below helps to develop that stillness. While all the eight steps are equally important, more attention is paid in the West on Āsanās and Prānāyāma only.

Eight-fold path of contemplation (Patanjali Ashtānga Yoga)

1. Yama: Responsible restraint, non-violence, truthfulness, non-stealing, moderation, detachment.

2. Niyama: Purity, contentment, austerity, study of scriptures, constant integrated awareness of divinity.

3. Āsana: Physical Postures.

4. Prānāyāma: Regulation of breathing.

5. Pratyāhāra: Withdrawing of senses inwards.

6. Dhārana: Concentration for 12 seconds.

7. Dhyāna: Meditation, 12 Dhāranās = 12x12 = 144 Secs.

8. Samādhi: Super conscious state, 12x12x12 = 28.5 Min.

Mind is constantly wavering. Like threads to the cloth, so are thoughts to the mind. Without thoughts there is no mind. Desires produce thoughts. Sealing on desires is one way to control thoughts. Another way is to exhaust the desires by fulfilling them, and in the process, taking care in not creating new desires. This is in effect burning the current Kārmic baggage and not create new baggage.

Thinking good, seeing good, hearing good, speaking good and doing good will minimize our thoughts and mind. GOOD is anything that unites us (Truth) and bad is anything that divides us (Untruth).

Serpent Power (Kundalini Yoga):

Kundalini Yoga is described in detail in the Yoga-Kundalini Upanishad which is a minor Upanishad. This is the eighty-sixth among the 108 Upanishads. It forms part of the Krishna Yajur Veda. This consists of three Nādis and seven Chakras in our body. Nādis are energy channels. There are three Nādis in spine:

1.   Yida (left)

2.   Pingala (right)

3.   Sushumna (midline).

Yida and Pingala correspond to sympathetic and parasympathetic nervous systems. Balance of Yida and Pingala Nādis is necessary for optimum health.

Sushumna Nādi in the spine, between Yida and Pingala, is supposed to be in a closed state at Mulādhāra Chakra. When mind is stilled and purity develops, this stillness acts as a suction force for the ascent of Kundalini energy.

The three knots are to be broken for Kundalini ascent:

1.   Karma   -   Kārmic baggage (Sthula)

2.   Kāma   -   Desire (Sukshma)

3.   Avidya -   Ignorance (Kārana)

This Kundalini energy is similar to the release of neuro transmitters (mediators/neuro-peptides) that give distinct experiences depending on the level of ascent in Chakrās.

Meditation

Seven Centers (Shad Chakrās + Sahasrāra) :

Chakrās correspond to nerve plexuses and endocrine glands and planets. The balance of these plexuses and secretions of the endocrine glands enables us attain optimum health status.

Sushumna is between Yida and Pingala in backbone and is usually in a closed state. The Kundalini power (spiritual power) is normally in a dormant state (as Ādi Sakti) and is coiled up like a snake at the lowest portion of backbone in Mulādhāra Chakra. Rāja Yoga helps the spiritual aspirant awaken the dormant spiritual power by opening the Sushumna channel. Through this channel the power ascends up from

Mulādhāra, gradually to Sahasrāra Chakra. When this ascent begins, the spiritual seeker starts having several spiritual experiences. When it reaches Sahasrāra on top of the brain, (union of Sakti and Siva happens) the person experiences oneness with creation. He becomes self realized and this is called Moksha.

Sahasrara chakra
Ajna chakra
Vishuddha chakra
Anahata chakra
Manipura chakra
Swadhisthana chakra
Muladhara chakra

Seven Chakras

1. Mulādhāra: Perineum, Mass (inertia), Saturn, Earth, Sacral Plexus, Testes/ Ovaries

2. Swādhishtāna: Pelvic Area, Movement (one-way), Moon, Prostate/Ovarian plexus, Adrenals

3. Manipuraka: Upper abdomen, Interaction (to and fro), Mars and Sun, Solar plexus, Pancreas

4. Anāhata: Heart area, Relationships (emotion), Venus, Cardiac plexus, Thymus

5. Visuddha: Throat, Vibration (speech), Mercury, Neptune, Laryngeal Plexus, Thyroid

6. Ājnā: Nasion, Light (Illumination), Jupiter, Cavernous Plexus, Pituitary

7. Sahasrāra: Top of Scalp, Consciousness (Prajnāna), Uranus, Pineal Body

"To succeed, you must have tremendous perseverance, tremendous
will. "I will drink the ocean", says the persevering soul;
"at my will mountains will crumble up".
Have that sort of energy, that sort of will;
work hard, and you will reach the goal".

Swami Vivekananda

7. THREE LEVELS OF SPIRITUAL PROGRESSION (THREE PHILOSOPHIES)

The three generally accepted philosophical expositions - Dualism, Qualified non-dualism and Non-dualism (Dwaita, Visishtādwaita, and Adwaita) are the philosophies that were developed by three different sages, Madhwāchārya, Rāmānujāchārya and Ādi Sankarāchārya. Some scholars think these are distinct and separate philosophies. However these three different philosophies are gradual progression of a devotee from Dwaita to Visishtādwaita, then to Adwaita while they progress in the spiritual journey.

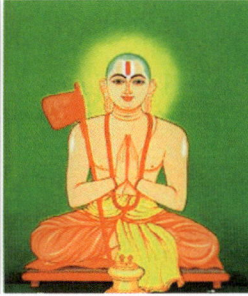

Madhwāchārya   Rāmānujāchārya   Sankarāchārya

"I am in the light" –" The light is in me" – "I am the light".

"I am the servant of God" –
"I am the son of God" –
'I and my father are One " -- said Jesus.

"Deha budhyā tva dāsosmi
Jiva budhyā tva amsākham
Ātma budhyā tvameva ahamiti
Me nistchaya matih" --- said Hanumān to Rāma

Meaning:

"When I think I am the body, I am your servant
When I think I am the mind, I am your amsa (devotee)
When I think I am the Ātma, I am you"
-said Hanumān to Rāma.

A. Dwaita: Dualism   Madhwāchārya
       (1199-1278)   Bhakti

B. Visishtādwaita: Qualified Non-dualism: Rāmānujā
       (1017-1137)   Bhakti

C. Adwaita: Non-dualism   Sankarāchārya
       (700-740)   Jnāna

8. TWO LEVELS OF CONTEMPLATION

From form to formless: In spiritual path, contemplation starts with the form aspect of divinity, since mind can only imagine divinity in a form. As Swami Vivekananda has observed, if a buffalo has to imagine God, it can only imagine God as a huge buffalo. As long as mind is involved, we can contemplate divinity in form only. As we progress in spirituality, we sublimate the mind (ego), and then we can contemplate on formless aspect of divinity as all pervading, all knowing, all powerful divinity beyond form, space and time.

'Form' (idol) represents ideal behind the form, like the flag represents the ideal behind the nation. Idol worship is indeed an ideal worship. Gautam Buddha was against idol worship, but his followers started

Sākāropāsana – Satyanārāyan Puja

worshipping his idol after his death. For Muslims it is the Kābā stone in Mecca and for Christians it is the Cross. These are all examples of form (idol) worship.

Initially people ascribe divinity to the idol and start praying **(Sālokya)**. As the devotee advances in spirituality, he feels kinship to the ideal behind the idol **(Sāmeepya)**. Then he starts seeing the ideal behind the idol in most of the things around him like Gopikās saw Krishna in the flowers, bushes, trees and everywhere **(Sārupya).**

As devotion reaches its peak of maturity, the devotee senses will be suffused with divinity. When he develops this inner vision, his whole world transforms into a beautiful divine tapestry. For him everything is divinity alone **(Sāyujya)**. This is the stage of "Sarvam Brahman", and called Nirākāropāsana.

Hence these two forms of worship are not exclusive, but are two stages of evolution of worship. While form worship is the beginning, the Nirākāropāsana is the final stage of this evolution.

 A. Sākāropāsana: -contemplation with form.

 B. Nirākāropāsana: -contemplation without form.

9. FOUR GOALS OF LIFE (CHATURVIDHA PURUSHĀRDHĀS)

There are four goals of human life according to Hinduism. Acquiring wealth in righteous means and desiring liberation from bondage. It is common during Hindu wedding ceremonies; the priest makes the groom recite "Dharmecha, Ardhecha, Kāmecha, Na Aticharāmi" which means that the husband declares that in pursuit of the goals of life called Dharma, Artha and Kāma, I will not violate my wedding vows. Pursuit of Moksha the ultimate goal is an individual personal sadhana; hence they do not say Moksecha in the mantras.

Artha and Kāma are to be attained by Dhārmic (righteous) means with the ultimate goal of Moksha (liberation) in sight.

A. Dharma: right conduct or righteousness

B. Artha: acquisition of worldly possessions and wealth

C. Kāma: satisfying desires for sense pleasures

D. Moksha: liberation achieved through God realization.

Spouse is referred as "Saha Dharma Chārini", meaning husband and wife are fellow travelers in the path of Dharma towards goal of Moksha. They help each other on this journey, while their common goal is Moksha. Thus Hinduism defines the best relationship between husband and wife as friendship to fulfill the four goals of life.

10. FOUR STAGES OF HINDU LIFE (ĀSRAMĀS)

Four stages of life (Āsramās) in Hinduism are designed for varying responsibilities at different stages of life.

First 20 years of life (0-20 years) (Bālya, Koumāra and Yavvana) is designated for celibacy and learning. Here the focus is on Brahmacharya - intense learning that results in developing character that shall lay foundation for rest of life.

The second stage consists of 40 years of life (20-60 years) as householder. This is an all important stage when they develop and support the family and society. The other three stages are supported by the householder.

The third stage consists of 20 years (60-80 years) where one becomes a hermit and spends 100% of time for service to society.

The fourth stage consists of the rest of the time in life after 80 years of age to be spent in full contemplation on God with a goal of Moksha.

For all these four stages, the goal is to reach Moksha. Initially by acquiring right knowledge, by serving a preceptor, then as a married householder by supporting the basic unit of society, then as retired person, serving the community and finally as Sannyāsi, through total renunciation of material possessions, attachments and union with oneness.

A.	Brahmacharya:	0-20 yrs	The stage of student.
B.	Grihastha:	21-60 yrs	The stage of householder
C.	Vānaprastha:	60-80 yrs	The stage of retired person.
D.	Sannyāsa:	>81 yrs	The stage of renunciation.

11. DHARMA: THE CONCEPT OF HINDU ETHICS

"Dhārayateeti Dharmah". The one that supports is Dharma. Dharma means right conduct. It is also moral or ethical duty. This is not same for everybody at all times. It varies depending on place, stage and circumstances. There are several levels of Dharma like the individual Dharma, family Dharma, societal Dharma, national Dharma and Dharma of mankind. Dharma of Cosmos is called "Rita", and is controlled by God.

One can sacrifice a lower Dharma for the sake of a higher Dharma, but not the vice versa. Buddha sacrificed the Dharma for his family for the sake of higher Dharma to the mankind, hence it was acceptable. It is not acceptable to sacrifice the society for the sake of family etc.

One's own conscience, nature and scriptures tell us about the correct Dharma at a given time. Highest Dharma of a human being is Ātma Dharma, i.e. to realize that he is Ātman. All other Dharmās are subservient to Ātma Dharma (Swadharma)

12. CONCEPT OF AVATĀR

Hinduism believes that there is a self corrective mechanism embedded in cosmos, when it is pushed to one extreme or the other. Similar to a pendulum pushed to one side moves back to the center, Dharma is the in-built cosmic order of creative intelligence.

Ten Avatārs of Vishnu

When this cosmic order is disrupted, sages and saints in the world pray for the descent of God into the world in human form to destroy unrighteousness (Adharma) and reinstate cosmic order (Dharma).

This descent of unmanifest, formless, attribute less God into human form is called Avatarana (descent). This Godhead in human form is called an Avatār. Among the Avatārs the ten incarnations of Vishnu are the most popular. These are the ten Avatārs of Lord Vishnu and are called Dasāvatārās:

Ten Avatārs of Vishnu

Dasāvatārās:

1. Matsya: the fish.
2. Kurma: the tortoise.
3. Varāha: the boar.
4. Nārasimha: the human-lion.
5. Vāmana: the dwarf.
6. Parasurāma: the angry man, Rāma with an axe.
7. Lord Rāma: the perfect man, king of Ayodhya.
8. Lord Krishna: the divine statesman.
9. Balarāma: elder brother of Krishna.
10. Kalki: the mighty warrior

Among these ten, Rāma and Krishna are the major Avatārās and are most popular. Many Hindus look upon Buddha as the Ninth Avatār in place of Balarāma Avatār. Several sages and saints are also considered as Avatārs.

Some people consider the ten incarnations (Avatārs) of Vishnu represent evolution of humans from aquatic fish, to turtle, to pig, to Nārasimha (half man and half animal) and finally to human. The purpose of an Avatār is to inspire, transform and liberate large number of people, to destroy evil and evil doers and uphold Dharma.

When an individual with purity prays, his prayers are answered. When group of pious people pray together for common benefit of humankind for long period, then God descends as an Avatār to correct Adharma and resurrect Dharma.

Lord Krishna says in Bhagavad-Gita

*"Yadā yadāhi dharmasya glānirbhavati Bhārata
Abhytthānamadharmasya tadātmānam srijāmyaham* Gita 4-7

(Whenever un-righteousness increases, and evil increases, I descend in human form on to the Earth to restore righteousness.)

13. CONCEPT OF TRINITY (TRIMURTY)

Absolute Godhead in the Upanishads is called Brahman (different from Brāhmana caste). This is also called Ādi Sakti. This Brahman was divided into trinity, depending on the actions performed by them. Brahma (different from Brāhmin, Brāhmanā and Brahman), Vishnu and Maheswara (Siva) with distinct functions for each one.

Brahma

Vishnu

Maheswara

Brahma:

He is the creative intelligence aspect of trinity responsible for creation of the cosmos. His consort is Saraswati, the goddess of education (cosmic intelligence).

Vishnu:

He is the creative sustenance aspect of trinity responsible for sustenance of cosmos. His consort is Lakshmi, the goddess of wealth.

Maheswara (Siva):

He is the dissolution aspect of trinity responsible for destruction of cosmos. His consort is Pārvati, the goddess of energy.

Apart from trinity each element in nature is represented as demi-god and goddesses. Earth is called Bhu Devi, water as Varuna, air as Vāyu, fire as Agni, space as Ākāsa. Similarly each direction of cosmos is represented by demi-gods called Dik Pālakās. Similarly all the planets in the solar system (demi-gods) are given a specific name.

14. TEACHER DISCIPLE RELATIONSHIP (GURU SISHYA PARAMPARA)

"Gu means Gunāteeta (above all attributes), "Ru' means rupāteeta (beyond all forms). One that fits this definition is God only. "Gu" also means Ajnāna (delusion) and "Ru" means destroyer. The one who destroys the spiritual delusion in us is guru.

Guru and Sishya are in each one of us. Sishya is our ignorance (Avidya or Māya). Guru is the Inner Consciousness (Ātman) in us. The external Guru directs our mind towards the inner Guru (Ātman) from whom we get illuminated.

Our day to day lives are like awake dream state. This means that we are awake to the world of duality which is really a dream state. The awakened state is Unity and Oneness. Guru enters into our dream state and wakes us up to the Truth (real awakened state).

> "Sraddhāvan Labhate Jnānam
> Tatparam samyatendriyah
> Jnanam labhdhva param santi
> Machirenādhi gacchati". Gita 4-39

(The one who has faith, steadfastness, intensity, control of senses acquires jnana. Through this Jnāna he experiences eternal peace very quickly).

In Guru-Sishya relationship faith and steadfastness (Sraddha) is of utmost importance. When a spiritual seeker reaches certain stage where from he cannot advance any further that is when one needs a spiritual preceptor. This preceptor is somebody who already walked the path and reached the destination.

It is said that when a disciple is ready (ripe) a Guru appears spontaneously. As eager as a disciple to get a Guru, so eager is a Guru to get to the right disciple.

My own personal experience confirms this. At a time when I reached a dead end in spirituality, I started looking for a Guru and visited several ashrams. However I was not satisfied with my search for a Guru. On October 1, 1989 Bhagavan Sri Sathya Sāi Bāba came in my dream as Uncle Sam (USA Army Recruiting Poster) asked me why I was looking for another Guru. Since then I accepted him as my Guru. He taught me mostly in dreams. Sometimes he taught as Dakshinamurty, where in all my questions were answered without opening my mouth in his presence. On one such dream he pressed on my ajna chakra and said that he was giving me vision. This was the beginning of enhanced intuitive vision of the scriptures and spirituality in general. Since then scriptures that I read became confirmation of this intuitive knowledge that I already experienced as revelation.

"When the thirst for liberation and the revelation of one's reality is acute, a strange and mysterious force in nature will begin operating. When soil is ready, the seed appears from somewhere! The spiritual Guru will be alerted and the thirst will get quenched. The receiving individual has developed the power to attract the giver of illumination. That power is strong and full". P 97. Sathya Sai Vahini.

This relationship is in-built in nature and is a highly sacred relationship.

"Tad viddhi pranipātena pariprasnena sevayā
Upadekshyanti te jnānam jnāninah tattva-darsinah". Gita 4 – 34

This means that "the self-realized souls can impart knowledge to the seeker because they have seen and experienced the truth. One should learn this Truth by approaching a spiritual master, inquiring submissively (in all your earnestness) and clearing doubts and by rendering service to him".

All the learning that occurs before a Guru appears is external knowledge that has not transformed into wisdom. Guru in his grace directs the vision of the disciple inwards and makes him experience the knowledge first hand and transforms the knowledge learned earlier, into wisdom.

In ancient times disciples used to live with teachers (Gurukulavāsa) and do service to teacher. In this intimate proximity and love, they used to do learning. These are like residential schools. However each Guru is like a university by himself.

While there are innumerable numbers of Gurus in the past, only a few are called Yuga Gurus. Each Yuga has its predominant Guru. The following are the Yuga Gurus of the four Yugas.

Dakshināmurty:

Krita Yuga is first of the four Yugās. In this Yuga, Dharma was stable on four feet. It is also called the Age of Truth. This was called the Golden Age without envy, malice or deceit. Majority of people followed Dharma. This is the Yuga of light and effulgence.

Dakshināmurty, the Yuga Guru of this Satya Yuga, was the youthful form of meditating Siva. He faces south and hence called Dakshināmurty. He was also called Ādi Guru. His silence transmitted knowledge to his disciples. His silence is his eloquence.

"Chitram Vata Tarormule,
Vruddha Sishya, Gurur Yuva,
Gurostu Mounam Vyakyhānam,
Sishyostu Chinna Samsayāh".

Dakshināmurty, the youthful Siva, was sitting under a banyan tree with older disciples (Sanaka, Sanāatana, Sanandana, Sanatkumāra, the four Mānasa putrā's of Brahma). Guru's silence answered all the questions of disciples.

This happens at times in the presence of elevated souls, all our questions disappear, without even asking a question. Their mere presence has a transformative effect on disciples. This was the experience of mine when I had come for clarifications of doubts at the feet of Bhagawān Sathya Sāi Bāba. Devotees of Ramana Maharshi also narrated similar experiences in the past.

Dakshināmurty

Dattātreya:

Tretā Yuga is the second Yuga. In this Yuga, Dharma was moving on three legs. This is also called Age of Knowledge. This was the age of sound (Pranava). Dattātreya was the Yuga guru for Tretā Yuga. He was the son of sage Atri and his wife Anasuya. He was supposed to be an Avatār of trinity (Brahma, Vishnu and Siva). He was the author of Tripurā Rahasyam, a treatise on non-dualism (Adwaita).

Dattātreya left home at an early age to wander naked in search of the Absolute. He seems to have spent most of his life wandering and finally attained realization in a town called Gānagāpur in Karnātaka in India.

Dattātreya was a baffling personality. Those who come to him with outer vision are caught in his Māya and judge Him as unfit to be a good example as a Guru. But whoever approaches him with reverence and faith, pierce through this delusion and gain divine knowledge. Sage Parasurāma and Kārtaviryārjuna were the disciples of Dattātreya.

He has taken several bodies as Avadhutās. The following are his Avatārs:

Sripāda Sri Vallabha,

Narasihma Saraswati,

Swāmi Samartha Maharaj of Akkalkot ,

Sri Vāsudevānand Saraswati,

Manic Prabhu,

Krishna Saraswati,

Shirdi Sāi Bāba,

Gajānan Mahārāj.

Recently Sathya Sāi Bāba and Ganapati Satchidānanda Swamy are also considered to be His Avatārs by some.

Dattātreya

Veda Vyāsa (Krishna Dwipāyana):

Dwāpara Yuga is the third Yuga. In this Yuga, Darma was running on two feet (righteousness is 50%). This is considered to be the Yuga of word. Sage Veda Vyāsa was considered to be this Yuga Guru. He codified the Vedās, authored Mahā Bhārata, Bhāgavata, Brahma Sutras and 18 Purānās.

While Veda Vyāsā is the author of Mahā Bhārata, he was also a member in Bharata dynasty; Veda Vyasa is also called Krishna Dwaipayana and is supposed to be 24th Vyāsa.

Veda Vyāsa

Ādi Sankarāchārya: (788-820)

Ādi Sankarāchārya

Kali Yuga is the fourth Yuga. In this Yuga, Dharma is running on only one foot (righteousness is 25%). This is the Yuga of action. Hence people have difficulty understanding the scriptures and epics written in Sanskrit by Veda Vyāsa. To solve this Ādi Sankarāchārya came in as a Yuga Guru. He founded four monasteries (Chaturāmnāya Maths), wrote commentaries in Sanskrit on several epics and scriptures written by Veda Vyāsa. He resurrected Sanātana Dharma and propounded Adwaita philosophy at a time when Hinduism was being run over by Buddhism.

Sankarāchārya wrote Sanskrit commentaries on most of the Sanskrit works of Veda Vyāsa, which constitute Sankara Bhāshya

Guru Sishya Parampara is well alive even today. The following is the partial list of most noteworthy Gurus in the Indian tradition arranged in alphabetical order.

They are:

A.C. Bhaktivedānta Swami Prabhupāda, Achārya Rakeshprasād Pande, Akhandānand, Amrit Desai, Ānandmurti Gurumā, Aurobindo, Bābā Lokenath Brahmachāri, Bodhānanda Saraswati, Bhagawān Nityānanda, Bhakti Tirtha Swāmi, Bhakti Caru Swami, Bhatrihari, Brahmānanda Saraswati, Brahmarshi Prem Nirmal, Chaitanya Mahāprabhu, Chandra Sekhara Saraswati, Gajānan Maharaj, Gorak Shanath, Goswāmi Tulasidās, Gurumāyi Chidvilāsānanda, Gopal Krishna Goswāmi, Gnānānanda Giri, Haridās Thākur, Hridayānanda dasa Goswāmi, Jayādvaita Swāmi, Jayapatāka Swāmi, Jiddu Krishna Murthy, Jnāna Dev Kabir, Lahiri Mahāsaya, Madhvāchārya, Maharishi Dayananda Saraswati (Founder of Arya Samaj), Maharishi Mahesh Yogi (Founder of TM), Mahāvatār Bābāji, Mātā Amritānandamayi, Meher Bābā, Mother Meera,, Muktānanda, Nāmdev, Nārāyan Dutt Shrimāli, Nārāyan Maharāj, Neem Karoli Bābā, Nimbārka, Nisargadatta Maharāj, Paramahansa Yogānanda, Purandaradāsa, Radhānath Sant Gnāneswar, Swāmi Rāghavendra Swāmi, Rām Dass (Richard Alpert), Ramakrishna Paramahamsa, Ramana Maharshi, Rāmānuja, Sādhvi Ritāmbharaji (Didi Mā),

Sāi Bābā of Shirdi, Sant Shri Āsāram Ji Bāpu, Sant Dhyaneshwar, Satguru Sivaya Subramuniyaswāmi, Satsvarupa Dāsa Goswami, Satya Sāi Bābā, Shāstri Nārāyanswarupdās, Sānkarāchārya, Shrirām Sharma Āchārya, Sri Ānandamayi Mā, Sri Aurobindo, Sri Chinmoy, Sri Nārāyana Guru, writer of Daiva Dasakam, Sri Sāradā Devi (female), Sri Yukteswar Giri, Srimanta Sankardeva, Sri Mātā Vijayeswari Devi (Female), Sri. Paripurnānanda Giri, Sri Paripoornānanda Saraswati, Sri Vidya Prakāsānanda Giri, Sri Viswamji, Swāmi Sathyānanda Saraswahi, Swāmi Nigamānanda, Swāmi Chidbhavānanda, Swāmi Chinmayānanda, Swāmi Dayānanda Saraswati (Founder of Ārsha Vidya Gurukulam), Swāmi Janakānanda, Swāmi Krishnānanda, Swami Lakshmanānanda, Swami Nigamānanda, Swami Niranjanānanda, Swāmi Rāma Tirtha,   Swāmi Rāma, Swāmi Rāmdas, Swāmi Satchidānanda, Swāmi Sathyānanda Saraswathi, Swāmi Satyananda, Swāmi Sivānanda, Swāmi Vivekānanda, Tamala Krishna Goswami, Tukārām, Upāsni Maharāj, Vallabhāchārya, Yogaswāmi.

Sathya Sāi Bāba: (1926-2011) :

A word about my Guru, Bhagawān Shri Sathya Sāi Bāba of Puttaparthi. He was born in Puttaparti, a small village in Andhra Pradesh, India. At a tender age of 14 he renounced connection with his family, parents and started preaching values of Truth (Satya), Right Action (Dharma), Peace (Santi), Love (Prema), Non-violence (Ahimsa) and Sacrifice (Tyaga). At a time I hit a dead wall in spirituality; he came in my dream on October 1, 1989 and commanded me to accept him as my Guru. Since then he was my Guru and he helped me develop intuitive vision of Sanātana Dharma and Spirituality.

Author with his Guru Bhagawān Sri Sathya Sāi Bāba

Bhagawān Sri Sathya Sāi Bāba brought the Vedic and scriptural knowledge to the door steps of common man in a very lucid form. All the "Vāhini Series" authored by him together with 42 volumes of "Sathya Sai Speaks" make significant contribution of spiritual knowledge to today's world. His service in health care, education and water supply is legendary.

In spite of internet, world wide web and Google, one still needs a preceptor for spiritual development and experience of divinity.

15. FOOD: VEGETARIANISM: SACRED COWS

Hinduism defines food as any intake that we take through our five sense organs, eyes, ears, mouth, skin and nose. All these sensory inputs are considered food. This food has to be holy and wholesome. More than what we eat through mouth, what we see and hear has a lasting imprint on our mind. Hence scriptures say, think what is good, see what is good, hear what is good, speak what is good, and eat what is good.

Indian Vegetarian Thali

Scriptures tell us that there are gross, subtle and causal elements to food. Allopathic medicine recognizes only the gross and subtle elements and has no concept that food has mind in it through the causal portion. The gross portion of the food is excreted as Mala (feces and urine). The subtle portion of the food is absorbed into the blood and become the gross body (flesh, bones, blood etc). The causal portion of food forms the mind.

This is why most Hindus do food prayer to sanctify the mind that is in the food. One of the three prayers is Brahmārpanam as follows.

Brahmārpanam Brahma Havihr
Brahmāgnou Brahmanā Hutam
Brahmaiva Tena Gantavyam
Brahma Karma Samādhinaha" - Bhagavad-Gita 4.24

This prayer invokes unification. It says that food is Brahma, is prepared by Brahma and offered to Brahma.

Prayer Aham Vaisvānaro is as follows.

Aham Vaishvānaro Bhutwvā
Prāninām Dehamāsritah
Prānāpāna Samā Yuktah
Pachāmyannam Chatur Vidham" -
Bhagavad-Gita 15.14

This prayer is a kind of assurance from Brahman. I am the Vaisvānara existing as gastric hydrochloric acid in all humans, am associated with inward breath (Prāna) and outward breath (Apāna). I will digest all the four kinds of food (swallow, chew, suck and lick) and purify them.

Harir Dāta Harir Bhoktā
Harir Annam Prajāpatih
Harir Vipra Sareerastu
Bhoonkte Bhojayate Harih.

Oh Lord Hari, you are the food, you are the enjoyer of the food, and you are the giver of the food. Therefore, I offer all that I eat at thy Lotus feet.

The state of mind of the farmer who harvested the food, the cook that prepared the food, the one serving the food, enters food. Plants thus have the least mind, animals have the most mind. Particularly animals going through the slaughter line experience fear, anguish. This state of mind gets into us when we eat that food.

People who are soldiers and athletes who need physical strength may benefit from meats. However, spiritual seekers who need a still mind are advised to eat only vegetarian diet, since it has the least mind. Foods that are too bitter, sour, salty, spicy, pungent, dry and burning should be avoided.

Sacred Cows:

Cows are revered species in India because of their utility in society. It is an expression of gratitude to an animal that give major share of its milk to us, useful for tilling the land, transportation and even in death, its skin is useful to us as shoes.

Sacred Cows

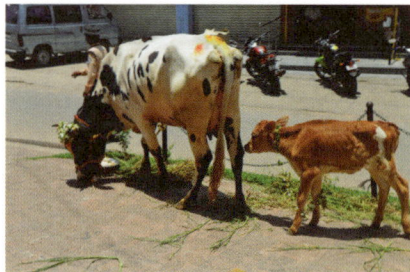
Cow and calf

This ascribing sacredness to cows is an expression of gratitude. This is similar to the West, where they eat most types of meat, but do not eat meats of domestic animals like cats, dogs or horses.

16. SECTS IN HINDUISM

There are several sects in Hinduism. Following are the predominant ones. Vaishnavates worship Vishnu as the supreme Godhead.

Vaishnavism

Savism

Saktism

Saivites worship Siva as the supreme godhead while Sāktites worship Ādi Sakti as the supreme godhead. While each one form of worship vary, they all in effect worship the same one and only supreme Brahman

17. OFF SHOOTS OF HINDUISM

Jainism, Buddhism and Sikhism are considered the off shoots of Hinduism. Some disagree with this assumption. Common to all these three off shoots are lack of caste system that is pervasive in Indian culture at the time. These came in as a reform at the time.

As time passes, people forget the real essence and significance of their religious practices and move to extreme practices away from essence. The Avatārās and the religious and social reformers come to enlighten people on the right and wrong of actions done in the name of religion and make them move to the essential aspects of religion. After the Avatārās depart and after the reformers die, people again move away to the other extreme from the message of the Avatārās and reformers. Then another reformer comes and tries to move it to the middle ground. This is an unending cycle. Many a time, these reformed practices become a different religion after the death of the reformer. This kind of reform movement took its name after the death of Gautama Buddha as Buddhism. So is the case with Christianity. These offshoots should be understood in this context.

Jainism:

Jainism was founded by Vardhamān Mahāvir between 9th and 6th century B.C. The earliest enlightened masters of Jainism were called Tirthānkarās and they were also referred to in the Rig Veda. At a time when rituals were dominant in Hinduism; Jainism and Buddhism came as reform movements against the rituals and sacrifices. Non-violence (Ahimsa) became the prime principle of these two religions.

Jainism promotes triple virtues viz., Right Vision (Samyak Darsana), Right Knowledge (Samyak Jnāna) and Right Conduct (Samyak Charita)

Great vows (Mahāvratas) of Jainism are Non-violence (Ahimsa), Truthfulness (Satya), Non-stealing (Asteya).

Jainism – Mahāvir

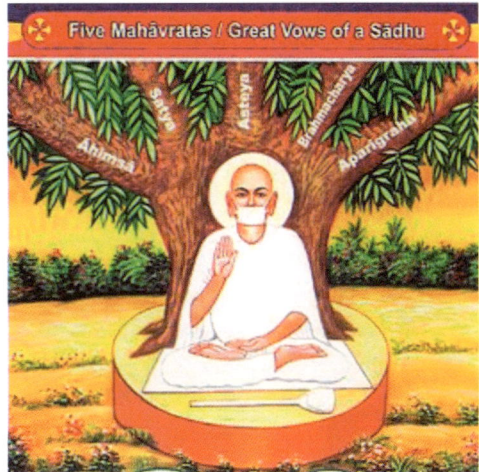

Jainism – Five Mahāvratās

Buddhism:

This was started by the Gautama Buddha (Prince Siddhārtha) around 500 BC. This was started as a reform movement against Hindu ritualistic sacrifices and caste system. After death of Gautama Buddha it became a distinct religion.

Tripeethaka, Anguttra-Nikaya, Dhammapada, Sutta-Nipata, Samyutta-Nikāya are some of the major scriptures of Buddhism.

Buddha taught four noble truths. These are:

1. Truth (Dukh) of suffering: Suffering is a fact of life.

2. Truth of origin of suffering: Desire (Itcha) and Craving (Trishna) are the causes for this suffering.

3. Truth of cessation (Nirodha) of suffering: Suffering ceases only with complete cessation of desires.

4. Truth of the Path (Mārga) to end suffering: Suffering can be ended by following Eightfold path (Ārya Ashtānga Mārga).

Budhism – Sāranāth Stupa

Buddhism - Celebration

These eight ways are Right Belief, Right Thought, Right Speech, Right Action, Right Livelihood, Right Effort, Right Mindfulness and Right Meditation.

Sikhism:

Sikhism was started in late 15th century by Guru Nānakji. He was a born Hindu and started Sikhism as a reform movement against prevalent practices of idolatry, ritualism and caste system. The word Sikh means disciple. Guru-Sishya tradition is well entrenched in

Sikhism. First Guru, Nānak Dev, Second Guru Angad Dev, Third Guru Amar Das, Fourth Guru Rām Das, Fifth Guru Arjun Dev, Sixth Guru Har Govind, Seventh Guru Har Rāi, Eighth Guru Har Krishan, Ninth Guru Tegh Bahādar, Tenth Guru Gobind Singh had all strengthened the Sikh faith.

While Sikhism promoted Hindu-Muslim unity in the beginning, it became a victim of Islamic extremism and intolerance. Several Sikh Gurus were killed by Islamic rulers. Fifth Guru Arjun Dev was killed by Jahangir, Ninth Guru Tegh Bahadur and Tenth Guru Govind Singh were killed by Aurangazeb.

It is the tenth Guru Govind Singh that promulgated that Guru Granth Saheb be their guiding scripture.

Sikhism - Musicians

Chanting the name of God (Nām Japna), earning by honest means (Kirat Kāro), selfless service (Vand Chakko) are the three basic tenets of Sikhism.

Sikhism – Golden Temple

Guru Gobind Singh (last living Guru) organized Sikh tradition of Khalsa (pure one). Male members traditionally wear 5 "K"s, uncut hair and beard (Kesh), comb (Kanga), traditional shorts (Kacha), wrist ring (Kada), sword (Kirpan). This was done to protect India from invading Islamic forces. Hence it created a warrior class to fight the invasions. This is the reason why Sikhism do not promote asceticism.

18. SIXTEEN VEDIC PURIFICATIONS (SHODASA SAMSKĀRĀS)

All these purifications are derived from the Karma Kāndās of Vedas. Sanctification of various acts from pregnancy to birth, development, and marriage to death is the goal of these Samskārās. Thus these worldly acts are sanctified for the higher purpose of life and living. There are sixteen such samskaras as follows:

1. Seemantam: This is a baby-shower given to a pregnant mother.

2. Bārasāla: It is Bālasāre. It is called Jātaka Karma. A sacred name is given to the child. Astrology of the new born is studied and horoscope is drawn.

3. Nāmakarana: Formal naming ceremony of the new born.

4. Anna Prāsana: Ceremony before giving solid food.

5. Kesa Mundan: Keshanta: First hair cut.

6. Chowlam: Karna-vedha: Piercing of ears done between 7-8th month.

7. Aksharābhyās: First alphabet was taught by the Guru.

8. Upanayan: It is called the 'the thread ceremony. The student starts studying Vedas from the Guru.

9. Nistchitārdh: Signing of marriage agreement.

10.	Vivāha:	Wedding. Marriage ceremony.
11.	Garbhādān:	First coming together of husband and wife for bringing conception.
12.	Sankhusthāpan:	Laying foundation-stone for a new home.
13.	Griha Pravesh:	Entering ceremony into the new home.
14.	Shashti Purti:	Celebrating completion of sixty years of age for the man of the house.
15.	Sahasra Māsa:	Kanakābhishekam: After completing 81 years of age, one completes vision of 1000 full-moon days. This is a celebration commemorating it.
16.	Antyeshti:	Last rites done after death.

Of the above sixteen, there are some regional variations on what constitutes the sixteen Samskārās. This is the way Hindus elevate their mundane, worldly social gathering celebrations into higher spiritual purpose, towards Divinity, Unity and Oneness.

19. HINDU MARRIAGE

In Hinduism marriage is an institution of union of man and woman. It is a Sacrament – a sacred commitment for a life long journey together (Saha Dharma Chārini) in pursuing right conduct (Dharma), prosperity (Artha), desire fulfillment (Kāma) and salvation (Moksha). Prosperity (Artha) to be attained by rightful ways (Dharma). Desire (Kāma) for liberation (Moksha) should be the undercurrent of this journey.

In the Hindu social system, marriage is not just between two people, it is also between two families for perpetuation of progeny and uplifting of society. It is the householder (Grihastu) who supports the people in other three stages of life (Brahmacharya, Vānaprastha and Sannyāsa).

Hindu Marriage – Fire Worship by Couple

Arranged marriages of earlier times have now moved into semi-arranged marriages with consent of parents, boy and girl. With women moving into work force, gradually the number of love marriages are on the increase.

Hindu Marriage – Pouring Saffron Rice

There are elaborate rituals in Hindu marriages that varies from region to region in India. However, the Magal Sutra Dhārana, Mangal Phera and Saptapadi are the most important aspects of Hindu marriage ceremony.

Circumambulation of the sacred fire: (Pradakshina, Mangal Phera):

After the mangal sutra dhāran the next important step is mangal phera. It consists of groom (Vara) and bride (Vadhu) walking around sacred fire four times clockwise. In the first three rounds groom leads the bride, while in the fourth round the bride leads the groom. Each round is done with reciting a sacred mantra and culminating into offering fried rice into the sacred fire.

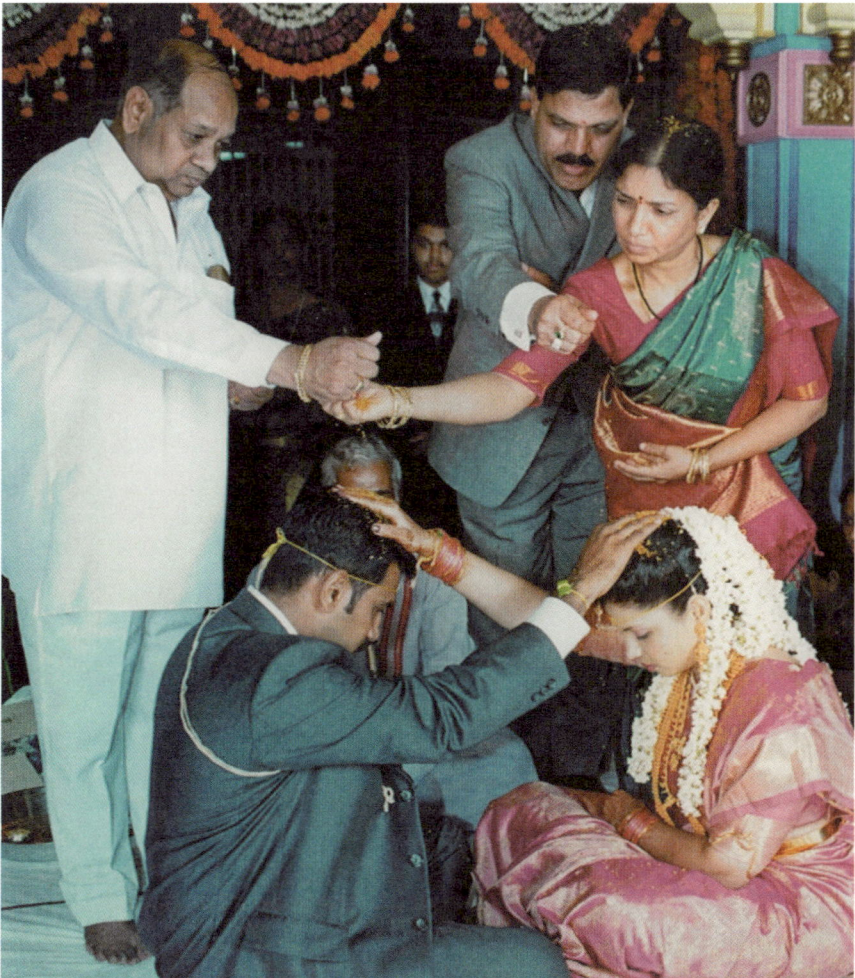

Hindu Marriages – Parents blessing the couple

In first round they seek God's blessings, in the second round they promise loyalty to each other, in the third round they promise to bring, protect, nourish, educate their offspring as good contributing citizens of society. In the fourth round the bride promises to uphold her responsibilities towards a harmonious family. This leads to the most important step in Hindu marriage the Saptapadi.

Seven Sacred Steps (Saptapadi):

This is the most important aspect of a Hindu marriage. Groom's scarf end is tied to the bride's sari's end to make a marriage knot. Groom keeps his right hand over the right shoulder of the bride. Seven rice heaps are placed on the Mandap floor. Each time they move the right foot forward first and bring the left foot to join the other foot later. Each time as the priest recite the Mantra, they step forward by stepping on the heap of rice. Seven such steps are taken. In the first three steps, the groom leads and the last four steps the bride leads the way.

First step:	Let us vow to share our food and physically strong together
Second step:	Let us vow to be mentally strong together
Third step:	Let us vow to prosper together
Fourth step:	Let us vow to be happy together
Fifth step:	Let us vow to have children together
Sixth step:	Let us vow to be comfortable with each other in all times
Seventh step:	Let us vow to be friends of each other.

Though there are various other steps in Hindu marriage Māngalya Dhārana, Mangal Phera and Saptapadi are the most important

20. HINDU FUNERAL (ANTYESHTI)

This is one of the sixteen important Samskārās. Practices vary from region to region. Cremation is done for the purpose of detaching the gross body from the suttle body. In general, the infants, un-married persons, sages and saints are buried. This is because, children, un-married youth, sages and saints have the least attachment between gross and subtle bodies. All others are cremated. There are four kinds of rituals of funeral.

Hindu Funeral – Body being carried

Hindu Funeral – Manikarnikaghat, Vāranāsi

1. Rites performed for people on the death bed (impending death).

2. Rites performed at the time of disposal of body (1st day).

3. Rites performed after the mourning period (13th day).

4. Rites performed in honor of the dead ancestors (annually).

Eldest son in case of father, youngest son in case of mother or others when there are no sons, perform these rites. Mourning period is from the 1st to the 13th day. These rites are meant for the release (transmigration) of the subtle body (Preta) from the gross body and its surroundings. Hindus believe that the subtle body along with the soul reincarnates into another gross body.

21. HINDU ICONOGRAPHY

Hinduism is rich with symbols and icons. These are developed with scriptural direction and as cultural traditions. Same symbols or gestures (Mudrās) may mean differently to different people of different regions. Some of the most common ones are detailed below.

OM (AUM):

OM is combination of A+U+M. It is the primordial vibration of creation. "A" represents waking state, "U" represents dreaming state and "M" represents deep sleep state and the silence between two OMs is Turia state. Similarly it also represents Brahma (creator), Vishnu (sustainer) and Maheswara (annihilator). It is also called Pranava (primordial sound). Creation started with OM and ends with OM. To go back to our source, which is our goal, we need to get connected on to the primordial sound. This is the reason why all Mantrās start with OM and end with OM. By meditating on OM and chanting OM (Pranavopāsana), it is said one can get back to their source and this is called Moksha.

Sacred Dot On Forehead (Bindi):

This dot is typically worn on forehead over the nasion (Bhrukuti - Ājnā Chakra), in between the two eye brows. Ājnā Chakra represents light and energy. It also represents Siva's third eye. Third eye is inward vision or intuitive vision. It is the Vision of Unity and Oneness where in all the diversity merges into Unity.

This sacred dot also represents Ādi Sakti (primordial energy). Married Hindu women wear this dot, to denote to the onlookers that they are the symbol of energy (Sakti); this symbolic dot transforms the lustful vision of onlookers into vision of reverence and respect that the women richly deserve.

Sacred Dot

Red Tilaka Powder

Sacred Ash On Forehead (Vibhuti):

Sacred ash has special significance in Hinduism. It represents end product of burning. End product of burnt human body is Ātman that cannot be burnt.

Sacred Ash (Vibhuti)

Ash represents Ātman. It represents impermanence of the body and permanence of Ātman. It tells us that the body that is made up of the five elements has to merge with the five elements in nature ultimately. This acts as a reminder to the wearer of ash and to onlookers of ash.

Siva Lingam:

Siva Lingam is a symbol of Lord Siva, the annihilating force in creation. Annihilation of the world of diversity into unity is Siva's responsibility. Anything that unifies is Sivam (auspiciousness).

Siva lingam is a double sphere that is round in all the dimensions. Thus it is a symbol of infinite Oneness. Form aspect of Divinity can be symbolized easily. Formless aspect of Divinity is difficult to symbolize. Siva Lingam forms the junction between form and formless aspects of Divinity; just as OM represents beginning of creative vibration. Hindus symbolize the formless Divinity with Siva Lingam.

Siva Linga – Vāranāsi

Siva Linga – Madhurai Temple

The lingam has also been interpreted as a symbol of male creative energy and the base of the lingam is considered female creative energy. World is a combination of potential (male) and kinetic (female) energies, positive (male) and negative (female) energies, yin (female) and yang (male), electrical (male) and magnetic (female). The world is Ardha Nāreeswara Swaroopam (a combination of masculine and feminine forces. When these are balanced, Unity remains, that is Sivam. Siva Lingam represents this Oneness.

Other Symbols or Gestures (Mudrās):

Sankhu (conch):   Represents primordial sound, creation, Vishnu

Damaru (drum):   Represents primordial sound, creation (Siva)

Chakra (disc):   Represents time, Kāla, Dharma (Vishnu)

Gadha (mace):   Represents destruction of evil (Vishnu)

Trident (trisula):   Represents annihilation of evil (Siva, Sakti)

Jap Māla (rosary):   Represents meditation (Dhyāna)

Palm Leaf bundle: Represents Knowledge, Vedas. (Brahma)

Kamandal: Represents fulfillment of desires, thirst

Veena: Represents fine arts, knowledge (Saraswati)

Lotus: Represents detachment, purity

Feet (Pada):   Represents support (Ādhāra)

Fire: Represents life energy, (Prāna)

Multiple Heads: Represents Omniscience, Omni presence (Brahma, Dattātreya)

Multiple Hands: Represents Omnipotence (Brahma, Vishnu, Lakshmi, Saraswati)

Blessing Hand With fingers up:
(Abhaya Hasta)   Protection (Abhaya), blessing

Hand with fingers
pointing down: Getting, receiving our impurities.

Lakshmi

Saraswati

Durga

Nataraja

Vishnu

Ganesa

Vehicles (Vāhanās):

Eagle (Garuda);	Represents flying mind, senses, desires (Vishnu)
Milky Ocean:	Represents purity (Vishnu)
Serpent (Ādi Seshu):	Represents mind, senses, desires (Vishnu, Siva)
Bull (Nandi):	Represents ego, animal nature (Siva)
Rat (Mushika):	Represents tricky mind and senses (Ganesa)
Swan (Hamsa):	Represents purity, discrimination (Saraswati)
Tiger:	Represents ego, animal nature (Durga)
Lion (Simha):	Represents animal nature, ego (Durga)
Peacock:	Represents colorful mind and senses (Kārtikeya)
He Buffalo:	Represents animal nature, ego (Yama)

22. DOCTRINE OF CAUSE AND EFFECT (KARMĀ THEORY)

Every action has a reaction. Every act has an effect either in this life or in future lives. Good actions will have good effects and bad actions will have bad effects. This works as Newton's third law "every action has an equal and opposite reaction". Some experiences of this life are the results of reactions from previous lives. Some actions of this life produce results in this life itself. Some actions will produce reactions in future lives. This is discussed in greater detail in the next chapter 23.

Say, 'This misery that I am suffering is of my own doing, and that very thing proves that it will have to be undone by me alone.' That which I created, I can demolish; that which is created by someone else, I shall never be able to destroy. Therefore, stand up, be bold, be strong. Take the whole responsibility on your own shoulders, and know that you are the creators of your own destiny. All the strength and succor you want is within ourselves.

Swami Vivekananda

23. DOCTRINE OF DESTINY

Doctrine of Destiny implies the belief in pre determination of events in life, brought forward from previous actions. Our birth is the result of Kārmic baggage from past lives. When this Karmic baggage is exhausted, it is called Moksha. The Karmic baggage we bring to this life is called destiny. This is our own making. We make our own destiny. "As you sow, so shall you reap".

While we have no control on the present destiny that was controlled by past actions, the future destiny is absolutely in our own hands. Our today's actions will decide the future destiny. This is why it is said that one's destiny is in one's own hands. Scriptures tell us three kinds of Karma that we reap the fruits from.

A.   Sanchita Karma:

The actions of the past lives, which are yet to produce results and will produce results at a future date are Sanchita Karmās. It is the fixed deposits of past lives that have maturity dates beyond this life, but in future lives.

B.   Prārabdha Karma:

This represents the past actions which produce results now in this life. It is the fixed deposits of past lives with today's maturity date.

C.   Āgāmi Karma or Kriyamāna karma:

These are today's actions that produce results in future lives. An Āgāmi Karma could produce results in this life if it is a "heinous crime. It is today's fixed deposit with future and occasionally immediate maturity.

Destiny - Prārabdha Karma

Among these three kinds of Karmās, Sanchita and Agāmi Karmās could be wiped out (burnt) by Jnāna or Self Realization, where as the Prārabdha Karma is inescapable. This is the reason why self realized souls like Sri Ramakrishna and Sri Ramana Maharshi suffered through worldly physical ailments.

Prārabdha Karma can only be burnt by going through it. God in His mercy hastens the experience of Prārabdha Karma for his devotees. He also anaesthetizes them from the suffering of Prārabdha Karma.

24. DOCTRINE OF FREE WILL: DIVINE WILL

Out of 8,400,000 species of God's creation, only humans are endowed with the Free Will to discover their source. They were endowed with the faculty of discrimination. They can function sub-normally as animals, being satisfied with eating, mating and sleeping or they can function to their full potential and use discrimination for higher purpose to realize who they are and be one with God, which is the sole purpose of this life.

So long as one has body consciousness(Ego), one has Free Will and hence accumulates Āgāmi Karma for which he has to reap results later on.

There is no Free Will for a person who functions in Divine Consciousness (Absence of Ego). He is totally surrendered to God and functions as a custodian of Divine Trust. He works with Nishkāma Karma, surrendering fruits of his actions to God. When one is totally surrendered (Sampoorna Saranāgati), there will be no free will. All that remains in this stage is Divine Will.

25. GOD'S GRACE

God's Grace is equal on all in the creation. He is never partial. He is only a witness. His grace is like the wind. We are like the boats in the ocean. The boats that have the biggest sails and the boats that have their sails unfurled catch more wind and sail faster.

Devotees are receiving instruments while God is the transmitting station. While the electromagnetic waves are transmitted to all, the devotees that have developed the strongest receiving instruments (purity of heart and stillness of mind) seem to receive the greatest volume of His Grace.

God's Grace is like sunshine that shines equally on everybody. However, the house that has its windows dusted, cleaned and curtains open receives more of it than the ones that have dirty windows and closed curtains.

26. THEORY OF REINCARNATION

After death the gross body mixes with the five elements (Pancha Bhutās) while the subtle body consisting of senses, mind, intellect and vital energy along with the Causal body, the Soul goes to a different plane of existence. Each plane of existence is called a "Loka".

Fourteen such Lokas are described. First six are higher planes and the last seven are lower planes of existence in relation to Bhu Loka (The Earth).

These are Satya Loka, Tapo Loka, Mahar Loka, Jnāna Loka, Suvar Loka, Bhuvar Loka, Bhu Loka, Atala Loka, Vitala Loka, Sutala Loka, Rasātala Loka, Talātala Loka, Mahātala Loka and Patāla Loka.

Higher Lokas:

Satya Loka, Tapo Loka, Mahar Loka, Jnāna Loka, Suvar Loka, Bhuvar Loka.

Middle Loka:

Bhu Loka (The Earth)

Lower Lokas:

Atala Loka, Vitala Loka, Sutala Loka, Rasātala Loka, Talātala Loka, Mahātala Loka and Patāla Loka.

Birth to Self-Realization cycle

The departed soul goes to higher or lower Lokās and goes through either pleasures or sufferings depending on their good Karma or bad Karma respectively on earth.

Reincarnation

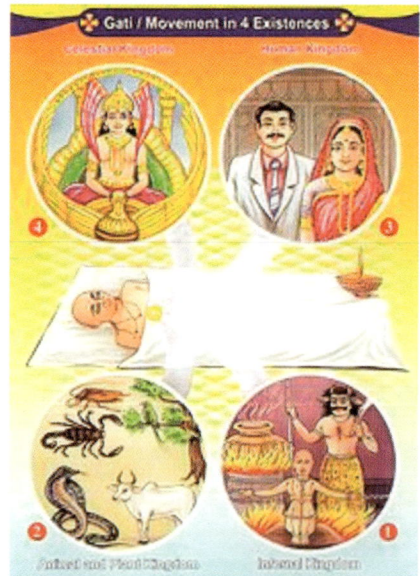

Journey of Soul

When a person dies with strong unfulfilled desires he will be reborn on earth after he completes the reaping of results of his previous actions (Karmaphala) in other Lokas. Reincarnation is also an opportunity to evolve to the full potential of human birth, i.e. Self Realization. After this, he will have no more pent up desires, hence no rebirth. He will be liberated and be one with the Ultimate Reality.

Birth Rebirth cycle - Reincarnation

This is the only way one can explain child prodigies who have illiterate parents and grandparents. This also gives hope for people who are good and pious, but did not reap the fruits of their labors in this life. No good ever done is wasted. No knowledge ever acquired is wasted. You always begin from, where you left off in previous life.

27. THREE NATURES AND CREATION (TRIGUNĀS)

World is Ardha Nāreeswara (combination of positive and negative energies) Swarupam (form). It is a combination of Spirit and Matter. The Spirit is called Purusha or Siva and the Matter is called Prakriti or Sakti. Siva is the Potential energy, while the Sakti is the Kinetic energy. If Siva is the electricity, Sakti is the magnetic force.

This Prakriti is composed of three intertwined subtle natures compared to the three strands of a rope. These substances are called Gunās (Guna in Sanskrit means a strand) and they are Gross (Tamo Guna), Subtle (Rajo Guna) and Causal (Sattwa Guna).

Vishnu – Brahma - Creation

Before the dawn of manifest world of plurality and diversity, there was unity. These three Gunās are in perfect balance and harmony with one another. When the state of harmony is lost the world of diversity is created.

Tamo Guna is inertia, inactivity, dull and stabilizing quality represented by Black color, Rajo Guna is activity represented by Red color, and Sattwa Guna is light, evolving and elevating force represented by White color.

Creation as a ripple in satchidānanda sāgara

While Tamo Guna causes confusion and causeless violence, Rajo Guna causes restlessness and bondage through attachment to the fruits of action, the Sattwa Guna gives spiritual progress. Going above the three Gunas (or balance of these three gunas) gives ultimate Liberation.

28. CONCEPT OF ILLUSION (MĀYA)

The illusionary force of creation

According to Adwaita School, there is only One and that One appears as many due to illusion created by God. This illusionary force, created by God prevents the experience of God, as Sun creates clouds and the clouds cover that Sun from view; the amber creates the ashes and the ashes cover the amber, the eye creates discharge in the eye and discharge covers vision of the eye.

Māya: Mala- Vikshepa- Āvarana: Sun's refection in the lake

Truth is the ultimate reality. Truth is defined as something that does not change with time and space. If we use this standard for all the things we see, feel, touch, nothing the senses perceive is fit to be true. The one that does not change and is beyond time and space is defined as Truth and God. Then what is the world we see, feel, and touch every day. This contemporary reality is called illusion (Māya). In order to make that single and simple 'white light' appear as many colors of rainbow, an intervention of a glass prism is necessary. This glass prism is Māya.

In order to make the One appear as many, the illusionary force was created at the beginning of creation. This illusionary force is called "Māya". This Māya has three characters detailed as below through which it blocks the vision of God.

Mala:

Clouding caused by impurities: cleared by Nishkāma Karma (Selfless Action) which causes Chitta Suddhi (purity of heart).

Vikshepa:

Caused by agitations in mind: cleared by Bhakti and Rāja Yogas (Devotion & Contemplation) that stills the mind.

Āvarana:

Caused by veiling and by covering: This is cleared by Jnāna Yoga (Knowledge). The Avidya (Ignorance) is removed by Sravana, Manana and Nidhi Dhyāsana.

Example: In order to see the reflection of the Sun (Ātman) clearly in a lake, the impurities in the water have to be cleared (Mala), the agitations of water have to be stilled (Vikshepa) and the covering leaves on the top of waters have to uncovered (Āvarana). When the water is purified of impurities (Mala), the agitations in water are stilled (Vikshepa), and the covering layers are removed (Āvarana), the reflection of Sun (Ātman) is seen clearly.

For a dreaming person, the dream is very real and he goes through all emotions of the dream characters in the dream. It is only when he wakes up from dream state, he realizes that all he has seen, experienced is unreal. Similarly for a realized person (Awakened Soul) this world is unreal and illusion (Māya). Likewise, this world of contemporary reality is the dream state of God. When he wakes up from dream, all that remains is, oneness .

Delusion will vanish as the light becomes more and more effulgent, load after load of ignorance will vanish, and then will come a time when all else has disappeared and the sun alone shines.

Swami Vivekananda

29. FIVE SHEATHS AND THREE BODIES (PANCHA KOSĀS)

Hindu scriptures describe three bodies the gross, subtle, causal bodies and five sheaths, the food, vital energy, mind, knowledge bliss sheaths..

1. Annamaya Kosa:	Food/Physical Sheath:	Gross Body (Sthula)
2. Prānamaya Kosa:	Vital Energy Sheath:	Subtle Body (Sukshma)
3. Manomaya Kosa:	Mind Sheath:	Subtle Body (Sukshma)
4. Vignānamaya Kosa:	Knowledge Sheath:	Subtle Body (Sukshma)
5. Ānandamaya Kosa:	Bliss Sheath:	Causal Body (Kārana)

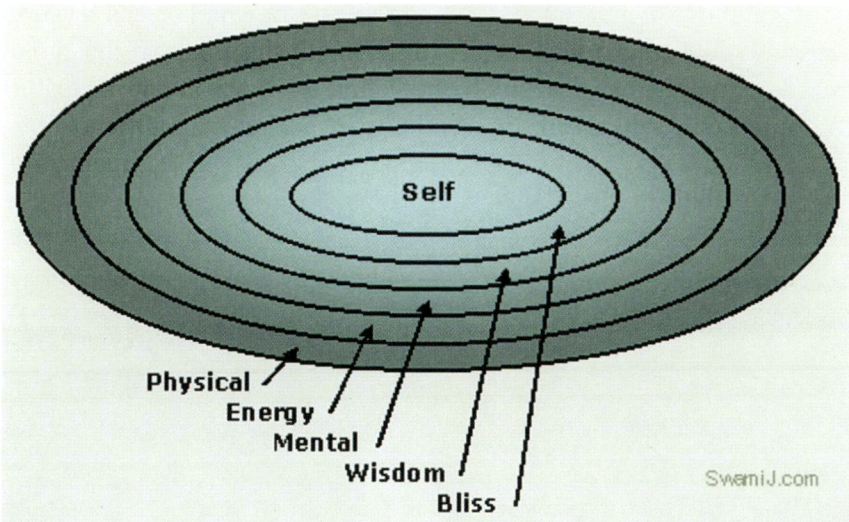

Gross body consists of food sheath (Annamaya Kosa) with bones, muscles, blood and flesh. It keeps changing from birth till death and disintegrates after death.

Subtle body consists of vital sheath, mind sheath and knowledge sheath (Prānamaya Kosa, Manomaya Kosa and Vignānamaya Kosa). This continues to live even after the death of the gross body. It goes to other planes of existence (lokās), either higher or lower.

When the soul reincarnates into another body, the subtle body-in-waiting along with the causal body enters into the new gross body. The Causal body (Ānandamaya Kosa) is our Truth. It is our permanent nature. It is this Causal body that remains with us during waking (Jāgriti), dreaming (Swapna), sleep (Sushupti) and deep sleep states (Turia).

30. ETERNAL COSMIC CYCLE (RITA)

Cosmos is in an eternal cycle of formation, growth and dissolution. It is in a cycle that starts from Unity (seed) to Diversity (tree), then back to Unity (seed). From God that is Unity, Primordial vibration (OM), three Gunās (three natures), Māya (illusion) are formed. Then five subtle elements (sabda-sound: sparsa-touch: rupa-vision: rasa-taste: gandha-smell) and corresponding five gross elements (Ākāsa-space: Vāyu - air: Agni - fire: Jala - water and Pridhvi - earth) are formed. From five gross elements the inanimate and then the animate world of plants, aquatic animals, amphibians, birds and animals are formed formed (from food prana came. With Prāna the life came into existent in all its various forms).

Then ultimately humans are formed as precursors of God. Among the creation humans are the only ones that have the capability to become one with God, since they are precursors of divinity. Rest of living beings other than humans advance through programmed evolution. They never violate Dharma. They act by built in instincts. It is only humans who are endowed with the faculty of discrimination (Buddhi). With this buddhi they have the capability to go against Dharma and pay the price of accumulation of Kārmic baggage (Pāpa) or follow Dharma, through intense spiritual practices (Sādhana) can advance to merge in Divinity and attain Moksha.

Hiranya Garbha (Brahma) is created from God as the embodiment of cosmic creative intelligence from His thought. With memory of the knowledge of creation of previous Kalpa, he creates the world. He lives for 100 years (Brahmā's). The life time of Hiranyagarbha is called Mahākalpa.

Krita Yuga	1,728,000 human years	4 x Kali Yuga
Tretā Yuga	1,296,000 human years	3 x Kali Yuga
DwāparaYuga	864,000 human years	2 x Kali Yuga
Kali Yuga	432,000 human years	1 x Kali Yuga
Mahā Yuga	4,320,000 human years	10 x Kali Yuga

1000 Mahā Yugās or 4.32 billion years is one day time (12 hours) for Brahma (Hiranyagarbha). At the end of each 12 hours is a deluge (Pralaya) occurs.

Sahasra yuga paryantam
ahar yad Brāhmano vidh
rātrim yuga sahasrāntam
te aho rātra vido janah".   Bhagavad-Gita 8 – 17.

The meaning of the Sloka is: "By human calculation, a thousand Mahā Yugās taken together form the duration of Brahma's one day, and such also is the duration of night".

2000 Mahā Yugās or 8.64 billion years is one full day (24 hours) for Brahma (Hiranyagarbha).

Brahma's life span is 100 yrs   = 100 x 365 x 8.64 billion years
                                   = 315 trillion 360 billion years
                                   = 315,360,000,000,000 human years.

At the end of one cycle (Kalpa) of Hiranyagarbha, the world undergoes dissolution and this is called Mahā Pralaya. Again this cycle of creation begins with a new exalted being born as Hiranyagarbha. Thus the process of creation, sustenance and dissolution goes on forever.

A straight line infinitely prolonged is a circle or cycle. In a cycle it begins where it ends and it ends where it begins. Everything in nature is cyclical. Seasons, Sun rise, Sun sets, civilizations, birth, growth and death are all cyclical. All the Nādi Sāstrās (Suka Nādi, Agastya Nādi etc) are based on this cyclical theory.

Growth has built in checking mechanisms. Osteoblastic activity (bone production) is balanced with osteoclastic activity (bone destruction) in bones. Creation in nature has a built in check called destruction that is followed by creation. This we see every year when spring comes when all the fallen leaves are replaced by fresh leaves. Death rejuvenates life. The universe goes through the same cycle as the seasons

31. CASTE SYSTEM IN HINDUISM (VARNĀSRAMA DHARMA)

This system of caste by birth is widely practiced in India even today. What is practiced now is based on birth and does not permit upward movement. The priest and intellectual class is called Brāhmin, the ruling class is called Kshatriyās, The business and farming class Vaisyās, the labor class is called Sudrās and the fifth class below Sudrās is called Untouchables or Harijans (as coined by Gandhi).

This practice has no scriptural sanction at any time. It is the vestige of community organization of old times when there were no management schools for the governing class to learn governance and no vocational schools to learn a trade for other classes. Hence these trades are passed from one generation to other generation from fathers to sons. It was the need of the times then that a potter's son became a potter and a shoe maker's son became a shoe maker. Later on a potter caste and a shoe maker caste were created based on the vocation of the families.

Today it has no place and needs change. It is not religion. It is tradition that needs to change to the needs of the current times. This change in Indian psyche needs to be transformed with the same vigor as slavery and women's rights in the West. Hindu scriptures give no sanction to this practice.

Krishna declares in Bhagavad-Gita:

Chātur Varnyam Maya Srushtam
Guna Karma Vibhāaginah   Bhagavad-Gita   4 – 13.

It states that all four castes (Brāhmana, Kshatriya, Vaisya and Sudra) are created by me based on their tendencies and deeds. It clearly does not mention that castes are determined from birth. It is the same classification of blue collar, white collar and executive class in the Western world.

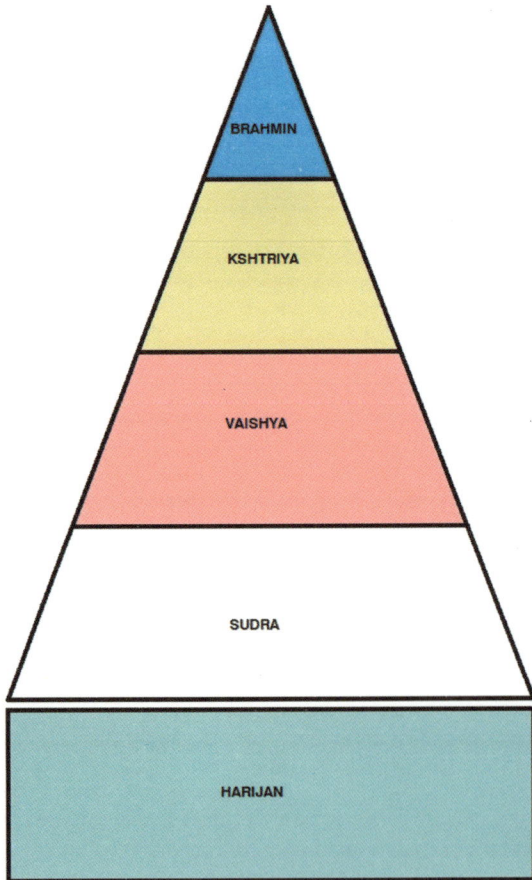

BRAHMIN

KSHTRIYA

VAISHYA

SUDRA

HARIJAN

CASTE PYRAMID

To go further, the Atri Samhita (Atri Smriti) 141-142: say

Janmānā Jāyate Sudraha,
Karmanā Jāyate Dwijaha,
Vedapathantu Viprānām,
Bhrahma Jnānantu Brāhmanāh. - Atri Samhita.

This means that by birth everyone is Sudra; by meritorious acts one becomes Dwija (twice born), by reading scriptures one becomes Vipra and by Brahma Jnāna (knowledge and experience of supreme) one becomes a Brahmana.

Brāhmanasya mukham āseet
Bāhoo rājanyoh krithah
Ooroo thad asya yad Vaisyah
Padabhyām soodro ajāyata
           --- Purusha Sukta from Rig Veda

The Brāhmins are the face; Kshatriyās are the shoulders; Vaisyās are the thighs and the Sudrās are the feet of cosmic person. They are all parts of the same divinity.

This clearly denotes that all castes are from divinity and they are differentiated only with the innate nature (Guna) and activity (Karma).

No religion on earth preaches the dignity of humanity in such a lofty strain as Hinduism, and no religion on earth treads upon the necks of the poor and the low in such a fashion as Hinduism.

Swami Vivekananda

32. SPIRITUAL JOURNEY

(Adhyāthmic Sādhana)

Spirituality is an uncovering process, evolving process and a spontaneous process. All of the creation and its creatures in the universe are in this journey to home from the day they were born until they die. They might advance some or retreat some in this journey. In each new birth they begin again where they left in previous life. They do not rest and are not fully and permanently happy until they reach the goal in this journey, i.e. becoming one with God. The difference between one and the other is that each one is at different station on this road, some ahead, some behind and ultimately, they all will reach the same destination.

It is like water evaporated from oceans form the clouds, becomes rain, form rivulets and rivers. Once they become a river, whether it is Ganges, Mississippi, Missouri or Amazon, their direction is only towards the ocean. They overcome incredible obstacles and finally merge in ocean. Once they merge in ocean they lose their identity as Ganges, Mississippi, Missouri or Amazon. It is called ocean and it acquires the universal salty taste of the ocean.

All living beings and everything in creation is in this incredible journey towards home, our starting point, like salmon fish in the oceans reach their breeding points (home) against incredible odds. Several species of birds and some sea turtles do the same. We are no exception. We started our journey from home (God) and will feel restless till we reach home. This 'home- reaching' process is the spiritual journey and the experience of the destination is called Moksha. The final home is called God.

As the rain rained in desert evaporates to form clouds several times, as rain rained into ponds evaporates several times and finally when it rained to become a big river, then only it reaches the ocean and merge. Similarly, we all take several births and re-births in this journey and in the final stage when we become the river (continuous spiritual flow called DHĀRA in reverse RĀDHA), we get blessed through final merger into our original source (God).

Hinduism talks about six hurdles in this path that one has to overcome. These are called Arishadvargās (Six enemies).

1.	Kāma	:	Desire
2.	Krodha	:	Anger
3.	Lobha	:	Miserliness
4.	Moha	:	Delusion
5.	Mada	:	Ego
6.	Mātsarya	:	Jealousy

While avoiding the above, a spiritual aspirant should promote in himself the Six positive qualities. These are:

1.	Satya	:	Truth
2.	Dharma	:	Right Conduct
3.	Sānti	:	Peace
4.	Prema	:	Love
5.	Ahimsa	:	Non-Violence in thought word and deed
6.	Tyāga	:	Sacrifice of ego, Selflessness,

He should follow one, two or combination of the four paths as below.

1.	Bhakti Yoga	:	Path of Devotion
2.	Karma Yoga	:	Path of Selfless action
3.	Jnāna Yoga	:	Path of Knowledge
4.	Rāja Yoga	:	Path of Contemplation

By eliminating the above six enemies (Arishadvargās), by promoting the above six human values, by following one, two or combination of above four paths, one can advance in spiritual path and reach the destination.

Character:

"End of education is character"- Sathya Sāi Bāba.

What we do right, when nobody is watching us, is character. Thus over a period of acquiring scriptural knowledge and doing spiritual practices, we should develop the character of truth, right conduct, peace, love, non-violence and sacrifice. In the boot camp of spiritual Sādhana, initially this comes through effort. As we mature and advance in spiritual path these values should be part of our character. Only then we will be spontaneously truthful, spontaneously Dhārmic, spontaneously peaceful, spontaneously loving, spontaneously non-violent and spontaneously sacrificing. These values become spontaneous and our second nature. They become part of our character. This character brings in the unending joy and happiness. The experience of this happiness (Ānanda) is called Moksha.

Scriptures serve us as road maps, to plan the journey, to get back on the journey when we get lost and also to monitor our progress in the path by looking at the milestones in the path. These mile stones are Equanimity, Peace, Joy and Happiness. If we are advancing in the path, we become less and less critical about others and the world. We experience more and more Equanimity, Peace, Joy and Happiness. Spirituality is not knowledge alone, but the experience of it. As we tread the path, we should experience the above milestones until we reach the destination, Moksha.

World Is A Mirror In Front Of Us:

We see ourselves in the world. If we see a terrible world and an unhappy world, it means that we are feeling terrible and unhappy inside. If we are seeing a happy and harmonious world it means we are happy and harmonious inside. Hence rather than putting efforts in reforming the whole world outside, a spiritual seeker needs to put more effort inside to transform oneself, in order to see a better world. World starts with us.

Any injustices we see outside should be used for introspection of ourselves and for reforming ourselves rather than judging others harshly. If you are discriminated based on color, race or national origin, use this insult as a stimulus for introspection and transformation. One needs to ask oneself whether he has ever discriminated others before for similar reasons, and caused pain to ohers. If the answer is yes, one should correct one's own attitude and behavior. Thus one transforms and evolves as a better human being, through spiritual Sādhana.

External nature is only internal nature writ large.
Swami Vivekananda

You have to grow from the inside out. None can teach you, none can make you spiritual. There is no other teacher but your own soul.
Swami Vivekananda

33. THE VEDĀS AND UPANISHADS

Sanātana Dharma stands on the foundation of the Vedas. The Vedas are the divine revelations (Apourusheya) and ancient and eternal (Anādi) beyond time, place or person. They are considered to have come from the breath of God. This means that they have come from cosmic vibrations (sound) and is perceived by the sages in their heightened states of awareness.

These are available as cosmic vibrations to be tapped by humans tuned in to their frequency in all times by all. This Vedic knowledge is freely available for all seekers of Truth. The only requirement is purity of heart and stillness of mind, with zero body-mind complex (ego).

When these conditions are satisfied, they develop capacity to tune into cosmic vibration. The all pervading cosmic intelligence (knowledge that is in the form of vibration) reveels itself to these seekers as revelation. This revelation is Sruti (what is heard through inner ear) or Veda.

Sage Veda Vyāsa classified this 'tapped cosmic knowledge' into four parts called Rig-Veda, Yajur-Veda, Sāma-Veda and Atharvana-Veda. Each of these Vedas have four parts, the Samhitas, the Brāhmanās, Aranyakās and Upanishads. They deal respectively with 1) Basic hymns, 2) Sacrifice rites specific duties, 3) Rites and Ceremonies and 4) Philosophy. They cover a wide range of knowledge relating to the Karma (action), Upāsana (contemplation) and Jnāna (divine knowledge).

If Samhitās are considered as the tree, Brāhmanās are the flowers, Aranyakās are the fruits while the Upanishads are the juice. Here is the essence of each Veda as described by Bhagawan Sathya Sāi Bāba.

Rig Veda: **Samatwam Rig-Veda Sāram**.

Essence of Rig-Veda is balance and equanimity. Lord Rāma represents these qualities at their best. Rāma, the embodiment of Dharma (Rāmo Vigrahavān Dharmah) is great example of equanimity.

Yajur Veda: **Yajnam Yajurveda Sāram**.

Essence of Yajur-Veda is Yajnam (Nishkāma Karma or selfless action for public good). Lakshmana adequately represents Yajur Veda by his selfless service.

Sāma Veda: **Pranavam Sāma Veda Sāram.**

Essence of Sāma Veda is Pranavam (contemplation on primordial source). Bharata is a classic example of this contemplation during Aranyavāsa of Rāma.

Atharvana Veda: **Sangham Atharvanaveda Sāram.**

Essence of Atharvanaveda is orderliness in society. Satrughna represents this essence.

This Veda describes how a human being can acquire special powers and mysteries by his own personal efforts and exercises, while in the other three Vedas, the mystery of Gods are described.

Activities like listening to discourses of sages and saints and reading scriptures are important. However, more important is self purification through which alone the true inner (Vedic) Reality is experienced. Till this happens our learning is not complete. This learning from the inner source (revelation) clears all our doubts. This alone is Veda for us in its true sense.

Hinduism is founded on this kind of foundation, Vedas. Veda is what is heard through inner ear (revelation). Once this inner voice is being heard, then all the further reading becomes confirmation of what is already heard. When the revelations begin, our knowledge transforms into firm wisdom.

Upanishads:

Upanishads are the end portion of the Vedas (Jnāna Kānda). Hence they are called Vedānta. Upanishad literally means "to sit near". It denotes sitting next to a Guru. These are composed from revelations to various sages in their heightened states of awareness. Hence these are called Sruti, the one that is heard (as revelation). All these are composed in Sanskrit.

These are considered to have been composed between 800-400 B.C. There were about 108 Upanishads, out of these 11 are considered to be Mukhya Upanishads.

They are:

1.	Aitareya Upanishad	-	Rig Veda
2.	Taittiriya,	-	Krishna Yajur Veda
3.	Katha Upanishad	-	Krishna Yajur Veda
4.	Svetāsvatar Upanishad	-	Krishna Yajur Veda
5.	Brihadāranyaka Upanishad	-	Sukla Yajur Veda
6.	Isa Upanishad	-	Sukla Yajur Veda
7.	Chhāndogya Upanishad	-	Sāma Veda
8.	Kena Upanishad	-	Sāma Veda
9.	Prasna Upanishad	-	Atharvana Veda
10.	Māndukya Upanishad	-	Atharvana Veda
11.	Mundaka Upanishad	-	Atharvana Veda

The subject of Upanishads is Ātman (Individual Self) and Brahman (Universal Self). It is the study of one Self, by knowing which everything is known. They also discuss about theories of creation of universe, about pancha kosas, mysteries of death and about Pranava (OM). This is the internal knowledge also known as Ātma Vidya. This is considered higher knowledge, lower knowledge being bookish and sastric knowledge. This is called higher knowledge since the source of this knowledge is Ātman/Brahman as revelation. This is also called secret knowledge, since this knowledge comes as revelation from within and books only confirm what is already heard. Some of these Upanishads, one from each Veda contributed the Mahā Vākyās. These are discussed in detail in the next chapter 34.

The goal of mankind is knowledge. . . . Now this knowledge is inherent in man. No knowledge comes from outside: it is all inside. What we say a man "knows," should, in strict psychological language, be what he "discovers" or "unveils"; what man "learns" is really what he discovers by taking the cover off his own soul, which is a mine of infinite knowledge.

Swami Vivekananda

If there is one word that you find coming out like a bomb from the Upanishads, bursting like a bombshell upon masses of ignorance, it is the word "fearlessness."

Swami Vivekananda

34. MISSION STATEMENTS OF VEDĀS (MAHĀ VĀKYĀS)

"Prajnānam Brahma" (Consciousness is God): Rig Veda

This statement is from Itereya Upanishad of the Rig-Veda. It is a Lakshana Vākyam (qualitative statement).

The consciousness which illuminates everything - that is God. This awareness is God. The consciousness through which the eyes see, ears hear, nose smells, tongue tastes, the skin feels - that consciousness is Prajnānam, that all pervading consciousness is Brahman. "Sarvam Khalividam Brahma" (all that is there is God only), "Sarvam Brahmam" (everything is God).

"Aham Brahmāsmi"   (I am God):   Yajurveda

This statement is from Brihadāranyaka Upanishad of Yajur Veda. This is an Anubhava Vākyam (statement of experience).

"I" am God. Who is this "I".

First stage:	"Aham Dehosmi"	(I am the body).
Second stage:	"Aham Jeevosmi"	(I am this mind).
Third stage:	"Aham Brahmāsmi"	(I am Brahman).

This "I" - that is in all stages of waking (Jāgrada), dreaming (Swapna), deep sleep (Sushupti) and super-conscious state (Turia) - is the real Aham. This "I" is God. When it is falsely identified with the body, it becomes ego (Ahamkāra).

"Tatvamasi" (That and you are one): Sāmaveda

This statement is from Chāndogyopanishad of Sāma Veda. This is an Upadesa Vākyam (statement of teaching).

You are that. That and you are God. You are also God. You are God only. Not only that I am God, you are also God. This shows the relationship of mankind to God. It shows brotherhood of mankind and fatherhood of God.

"Ayamātma Brahma" (This Ātma is God)   Atharvanaveda

This statement is from Māndukyopanishad of Atharvana Veda. This is a Sakshātkār Vākyam (statement of realization).

This Ātma is God. This Ātma that is separate from body is Brahman. God is "Sarva Bhootātma" (God is indweller of all beings) and "Sarva Bhootāntarātma" (God lives as an indweller on all hearts). "Isvara Sarva Bhutānām" (God is in all beings).

These Mahā Vākyās express the highest truths to contemplate. 'Yad Bhāvam Tat Bhavati", meaning that whatever we continuously think, we become that. By contemplating on these truths, we become Brahman, who we really are.

35. CASE HISTORIES OF VEDĀS (PURĀNĀS)

The esoteric truths expressed in Vedās are difficult for the average people to understand. To make it easy for the lay person to know about them, the Purānas are written. Through stories the same essence of Vedas is brought to the level of average intellect by Veda Vyāsa in the form of Purānas. Most popular ones are eighteen Purānas. They add up to 400,000 Slokas, equivalent to four Mahā Bhāratās.

They are Agni, Bhāgavata, Bhavisya, Brahma, Brahmānda, Brahmavaivarta, Garuda, Kurma, Linga, Mārkandeya, Matsya, Nārada, Padma, Skānda, Vāmana, Varāha, Vāyu, and Vishnu Purānas.

Several of Vratās practiced by Hindus come from these Purānas. The most common Vratā, the Hindus perform is the "Satyanārāyana Vratā" that comes from Skānda Purāna. Veda Vyāsa summarized the essence of these eighteen Purānas as -

Ashtādasa purāneshu vyāsena vachanam dwayam,
paropakāraya punyaya, pāpāya para pedanam".

This means "Help Ever – Hurt Never".

Bhāgavata Purāna: Srimad Bhāgavatam:

Its primary focus is on Bhakti (devotion) to all the incarnations of Lord Vishnu (Sustainer aspect of trinity), in particular towards Krishna. This text is in Sanskrit, written by sage Veda Vyāsa after completing Mahā Bhārata, Brahma Sutras. It is said that Vyāsa's mind was greatly agitated even after writing Mahā Bhārata and Brahma Sutrās. He sought direction from sage Nārada (celestial sage, the son of Brahma, the creative aspect of Trinity) and Nārada advised him to write Bhāgavatam.

Krishna lifting Goverdhana

Vishnu blessing Dhruva

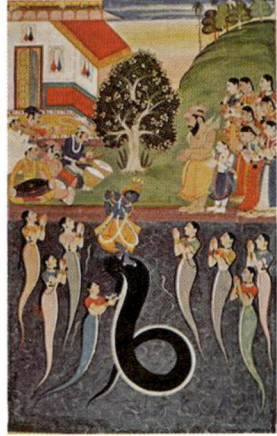
Krishna - Kaliya

It is said to be unending, since the lives of devotees still continue to this day. Veda Vyāsa ultimately experienced peace after completing Srimad Bhāgavatam.

Bhāgavatam consists of twelve Skandas (chapters) in about 18,000 verses. It includes several stories of the Avatārās of Vishnu and the life of Krishna. This was the first Purāna translated into French three times between 1840 and 1857. It takes the form of recounting Vyāsā's work, by his son sage Suka to Parikshit, the grandson of Arjuna and son of Abhimanu. Parikshit was cursed by sage Sringi, to die in seven days. Prior to his death, King Parikshit approached sage Suka (son of Vyāsa), seeking the ways of Salvation. Sage Suka narrated Bhāgavata Purāna for seven days and after listening to the sage, Parikshit acquires state of Moksha.

36. SIX SCHOOLS OF HINDU PHILOSOPHY (SHAD DARSANĀS)

Hindu sages at different periods of time developed six different schools of philosophy called Darsanas. Vyāsā's Uttara Mimāmsa is also called Brahma Sutra which is one of the Prasthāna Traya. The other two of Prasthāna Traya are Upanishads and Bhagavad-Gita. Following are the six different schools of philosophies.

1. Sāmkhya school   : by Kapila
2. Purva Mimāmsa School   : by Jaimini
3. Uttar Mimāmsa School   : by Vyāsa
4. Yoga School   : by Patanjali
5. Nyāya School   : by Gowtama
6. Vaiseshika School   : by Kanāda

Each soul is potentially divine. The goal is to manifest this divinity within, by controlling nature, external and internal. Do this either by work, or worship, or psychic control, or philosophy — by one, or more, or all of these — and be free. This is the whole of religion. Doctrines, or dogmas, or rituals, or books, or temples, or forms, are but secondary details.

Swami Vivekananda

37. ĀGAMĀS: CODE OF WORSHIP AND CONSTRUCTION OF TEMPLES

Āgamās deal with prayers and rituals connected to construction of temples and worship of idols. Āgamās deal with –

1. The philosophy and spiritual knowledge behind the worship of the deity,

2. The Yoga and mental discipline required for this worship,

3. The specific rituals of worship offered to the deity.

Each Āgamā consists of four parts.

The **first part** includes the philosophical and spiritual knowledge.

The **second part** covers the Yoga and the mental discipline.

The **third part** specifies rules for the construction of temples and for sculpting and carving the idols of deities for worship in the temples.

The **fourth part** of the Āgamās includes rules pertaining to the observances of religious rites, rituals, and festivals.

There are three kinds of Āgamās based on principal deity. These are: Saiva Āgamās, Vaishnava Āgamās and Sākteya Āgamās.

38. THE HINDU EPICS (ITIHASĀS)

Rāmāyana and Mahā Bhārata are the two great epics of India. Bhagavad-Gita, the most revered scripture of Hindus is part of Mahā Bhārata.

Rāmāyana:

Rāmāyana is known as Ādi Kāvya (first literary treatise). It is the story of Rāma, the Avatār of Vishnu. The Epic is written by Vālmiki in Sanskrit. Rāma + Ayana = Rāmāyana means Rāma's journey. It consists of 24,000 verses in seven books, called Kāndās and 500 cantos called Sargās. These are Bāla Kānda, Ayodhya Kānda, Aranya Kānda, Kishkinda Kānda, Sundara Kānda, Yuddha Kānda and Uttara Kānda. Each Kānda is again divided into small sections called Sargās.

It is later translated into all major Indian and other languages of the world. In addition, there are several other versions of Rāmāyanās written in various Indian regional languages by several authors.

Rāma's Coronation   Rāma, Lakshmana , Sita   Rāma's anger at Sāgara

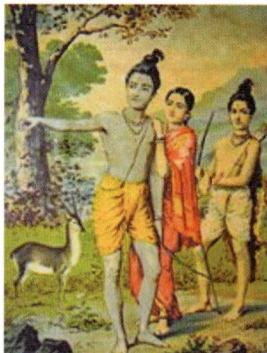

Sanskrit Versions:

1. Srimad Vālmiki Rāmāyan : Authoured by Vālmiki

2. Adhyātma Rāmāyana : by Vyāsa
   Brahmānda Purāna

3. Yoga Vāsishta : Ascribed to Vāmiki.

4. Ānanda Rāmāyana : Attributed to Vālmiki.

5. Agastya Rāmāyana : Attributed to Vālmiki

6. Adbhuta Rāmāyana : Attributed to Vālmiki.

POPULARITY OF REGIONAL RAMAYANAS

TULSIDAS (1574)

PREMANAND 17TH

KRTTIVAS 14TH c

SRIDHARA 18TH c.

BALARAMA DAS 16TH c.

RANGANATHA 12TH - 15TH c.

NARAHARI 16TH c.

KAMBAN 11TH c.

ELUTTACAN 17TH

Regional Language Versions:

1. Assamese: Saptakānda Rāmāyana or Kotha Rāmāyana –
    14th century - by Madhava Kandali.

2. Bengali: Krittivasi Rāmāyana - 15th century –
    by Krittibas Ojha.

3. Gujarati: Tulsi-Krta Rāmāyana - 17th century - (adaptation
    of Rāmcharit Manas) - by Premānand Swami.

4. Hindi: Rāmacharitmanas - 16th century –
    by Goswāmi Tulasi Das.

5. Kannada: Kumudendu Rāmāyana - 13th century
    Rāmachandra Charita Purāna - 13th century –
    by Nagāchandra.
    Kumāra-Valmiki Torave Rāmāyana - 16th century
    - Narahari

6. Kashmiri: Rāmāvatāra Charita, in 19th century.

7. Konkini: Rāmāyanu - 15th century - by Krishnadāsa Shama

8. Malayalam: Adhyātma Rāmāyanam Kikipattu - 16th century –
    by Thunchaththu Ezhuthac

9. Marathi: Bhavartha Rāmāyana - 12-13th century -
    by Eknāth.

10. Nepali: Bhānubhakta Rāmāyana - 19th century –
    by Bhānubhakta Ācharya.
    Nepal Bhasa Siddi Rāmāyan - 20th century –
    by Siddhidas Mahaju.

11. Oriya: Dandi Rāmāyana or Jagamohan Rāmāyana –
    16th century - by Balarām Dās.

12. Tamil: Kamba Rāmāyanam - 12th century - by Kamban.

13. Telugu: Sri Ranganādha Rāmāyanam - 13th century –
               by Buddhā Reddy.
               Bhāskara Rāmāyanam - 14th century -
               by Hulakki Bhāskar.
               Molla Rāmāyanam - 15th century -
               by Kummara Molla.

14. Urdu: Pothi Rāmāyana - 17th century – by Chucklustha

International Versions:

1. Burma   Yamayana

2. Cambodia   Reamker

3. Thailand: Ramakien

4. Laos: Phra   Lak Phra Lam

5. Malaysia: Hikayat Seri Rāmā

6. Java & Indonesia: Kakawin Rāmāyana

7. Philippines: Rajah Magandini

8. Nepal: Siddhi Rāmāyan and
                      Bhanubhaktako Rāmāyan

"Rāmo Vigrahavān Dharmah".

Rāma is the embodiment of Dharma. Rāma showed through his life how to be an ideal son, ideal student, ideal spouse, ideal brother, ideal son and an ideal king. Rāmāyan depicts ideal relationships between parents and sons, between brothers, between friends, between devotee and divinity. Rāmāyan projects human values and the concept of Dharma.

Mahā Bhārata:

Mahā Bhārata is the longest Sanskrit epic written by sage Veda Vyāsa. It has 100,000 Slokas and about 1.8 million words. Bhagavad-Gita is part of the Mahā Bhārata. It is divided into 18 Parvas. Each Parva has many sub-parvas.

1.	Ādi Parva	10.	Sauptika Parva
2.	Sabhā Parva	11.	Stri Parva
3.	Vana Parva	12.	Sānti Parva
4.	Virāta Parva	13.	Anusāsana Parva
5.	Udyoga Parva	14.	Ashvamedhika Parva
6.	Bhishma Parva	15.	Āshramavāsika Parva
7.	Drona Parva	16.	Mausala Parva
8.	Karna Parva	17.	Mahāprasthanika Parva
9.	Salya Parva	18.	Svargārohana Parva.

Kurukshetra war depiction in Mahābhārata manuscript

Veda Vyāsa, was the grandfather of the heroes of the Mahā Bhārata. He narrated the epic to his son Suka and to his disciple Vaisampāyana.

Vaisampāyana narrated the epic to Janamejaya (son of Parikshit and great grandson of Arjuna) during performance of a great sacrifice. Sage Suta narrated the same epic to Janmejaya, sage Saunaka and others later.

It starts with birth and upbringing of Kauravās and Pāndavās: life at the Kaurava court and the game of dice: twelve years of exile in the forest for Pāndavās: one year of exile in disguise of Pāndavās at Virāta court: preparations for the great war: first part of great battle with Bhishma as commander-in-chief for Kauravās: The battle with Drona as commander: Karna as commander: last part of the battle with Salya as commnder: murder of sleeping Upa-Pandavās (Pāndavā children) by Aswatthāma: Gāndhari and other Kauravā women lament the death of the Kauravas: crowning of Dharmarāja: final instructions of Bhishma: Ashwamedha conducted by Dharmarāja: Dhritarashtra, Gandhāri and Kunti leave for forest and their death in forest: civil war between Yadavās with maces (Musalam) and death of Lord Krishna: final journey (Mahā Prasthāna) of Pāndavās: Pāndavās return to spiritual domain (Swarga Loka).

39. BHAGAVAD-GITA

(The essence of Upanishads)

The holiest book of Hindus is Bhagavad-Gita. It is in the Sixth chapter, Bhishma Parva of Mahābhārata. It is a narration by Sanjaya, the charioteer to Dhritarāshtra, the father of Kauravās in a form of dialogue between them.

The Upanishads are the knowledge portion of Vedās. The Bhagavad-Gita is considered as the essence of all the Upanishads. This is the most revered scripture of the Hindus. Gita has 701 Slokas in 18 chapters called Yogas. They are:

1.   Arjuna Vishāda Yoga
2.   Sānkhya Yoga
3.   Karma Yoga
4.   Jnāna Yoga
5.   Karma Sannyāsa Yoga
6.   Ātma Samyama Yoga
7.   Vijnāna Yoga
8.   Akshara Parabrahma Yoga
9.   Rāja Vidyā Rāja Guhya Yoga
10.   Vibhuti Yoga
11.   Viswarupa Sandarsana Yoga
12.   Bhakti Yoga
13.   Kshetrakshetragna Vibhāga Yoga
14.   Guna Traya Vibhāga Yoga
15.   Purushottama Prāpti Yoga
16.   Daivāssura Sampat Vibhāga Yoga
17.   Sraddhā Traya Vibhāga Yoga
18.   Moksha Sannyāsa Yoga

Dharmakshetram:

Dharmakshetre Kurukshetre
Samaveta yuyutsavah
Māmakāh pāndavaschiva
kimakurvata Sanjaya   Gita   1-1

The Bhagavad-Gita starts with the word Dharmakshetre in the first Sloka: This Dharmakshetra (Consciousness) is in every one of us in which there is an ongoing battle of Kurukshetra (discrimination of good and bad). In this battle the evil forces are represented by 100 Kauravas and good forces are represented by 5 Pāndavas. Through surrender to Lord Krishna and through his guidance, the charioteer of Arjuna, the good forces vanquish the evil forces.

Role of Compassion (Daya):

Arjuna, the great warrior of the Pāndavās was an angry man, filled with hatred and thoughts of revenge to kill Kauravās, his arch rivals. Through his valor and through great personal sacrifices, he acquired multiple warheads. Before the starting of the Kurukshetra battle, his mind was predominantly filled with extreme anger, hatred and revenge against them.

Krishna and Arjuna in Chariot in Kurukshetra War

However, when he arrived at the battlefield, instead of seeing rivals in Kauravās, he saw his cousins, friends, teachers, fathers and grandfathers. His mind was moved to the other extreme, from anger and revenge to extreme compassion and self guilt. Once this compassion was born in the heart of Arjuna, he became eligible to receive Jnāna (Bhagavad-Gita). Krishna and Arjuna were relatives and true friends. There were ample opportunities between them to receive the same truths before the war.

However Arjuna's mind was not conducive to receive Gita because of anger, hatred and revenge. The moment compassion dawned in (other extreme), he became eligible to receive Gita. The purpose of Gita is to bring people to middle path (Buddhā's Madhye Mārga). After teaching Gita, Arjuna moved from the extremes of anger, hatred and revenge on one side and compassion, love and pity on the other side to the middle ground, where 'duty' became predominant above both these emotions.

This middle ground is 'non attached right action to protect Dharma'. After receiving the sermon of Gita from Lord Krishna, Arjunā's mind changed in tune with his consciousness (Krishna). He was able to practice Mama Dharma/ Swadharma (Ātma Dharma) and, which is above all other Dharmās.

Mama Dharma:

As has already been indicated, the First Sloka of Gita starts with Dharmakshetre as follows:

> **Dharma**kshetre Kurukshetre Samaveta yuyutsavah
> Māmakāh pāndavaschiva kimakurvata Sanjaya
>
> Gita   1-1

The Gita ends with the last Sloka as follows:

> Yatra Yogeeswara Krishno
> yatra Partho dhanurdharah
> Tatra srir vijayor bhutir dhruvā
> nitir matir **mama**"   Gita   18-78

The essence of Bhagavad-Gita, sages say, is summarized by the last word in the last Sloka and the first word in first Sloka. Mama + Dharma = Mama Dharma (Consciousness). So the essence of Gita is Ātma Dharma.

Mamakār: Me and Mine:

Selfishness, attachment to me and mine (Mamatva, Mamakār) is the root cause of self destruction. In the very first Sloka of Bhagavad-Gita, Dhritarāshtra, the father of Kauravās differentiates between his children (Kauravās) and his brother Pāndu's children (Pandavās) by using the word MĀMAKĀH. This Mamatva is the seed for self destruction of Kaurava clan in Kurukshetra war.

> *Dharmakshetre Kurukshetre Samaveta yuyutsavah*
> *Māmakāh pāndavaschiva kimakurvata Sanjaya*
>
> Gita   1-1

Sacrifice of selfishness (Swārdha Tyāga) is a high road for self realization.

Gita's first Sloka shows this selfishness with word "Māmakāh", and the last Sloka of Gita talks about surrender to Divine will. Surrender to Divine will is surrender of limitedness (selfishness).

One Sloka Gita (Eka Sloki Gita):

> *Yatra Yogeeswarah Krishno*
> *Yatra Pārdho Dhanurdharah*
> *Tatra Sri Vijayo Bhutir*
> *dhruvā nitir matir mama".*   18-78

"Wherever Krishna, the Yogeeswara and the Arjuna the archer, ready to fight, are there together, there will be prosperity, victory, fame and morality".

Prosperity, victory, fame and morality follow the surrendered (to Ātma- Krishna) Dharmic action (Arjuna).

Anchor Slokas of the Gita:

Kārpanya Doshopahata swabhāvah
Pricchāmi tvām dharma sammudha chetāh
Yacchreyāh ssyā nnischitam bruhi tanme
Sishyaste ham sādhi mām tvam prapannam".   Gita 2-7

After lecturing and reasoning with Krishna, finally Arjuna surrenders to Krishna and asks for guidance in further action. In this Sloka, Arjuna surrenders to Krishna. "My heart is overpowered by compassion. My mind is confused to identify my duty. I ask thee. Tell me decisively what is good for me. I am thy disciple. I surrendered to you fully. Instruct me on my duty.

Ananyāschinta Yantomām
ye janāh paryupāsate
Teshām nityābhi yuktānām
Yogah kshemam vahāmyaham".   Gita 9-22.

"Those that worship me with single-mindedness, think of me alone, those ever self controlled, I secure for them that is not already possessed (Yoga) by them and preserve for them the things they already possess (Kshema). This is Krishna's promise.

Sarva Dharmān Parityajya
Māmekam saranam vraja
Aham tvā sarva pāpebhyo
Moksha ishyāmi māsuchah".   Gita 18-66

"Abandon all Dharmās (of body, mind and intellect) and take refuge in me alone (Ātma Dharmā); I will liberate thee from all sins; grieve not". This is Krishna's Guarantee.

Sorrow (Vishāda) role in spiritual growth:

Sorrow (Vishāda) is a big contributor for hastening the inward spiritual journey. When everything is going well, few people think about Moksha. When going gets rough, people's mind turns inward. That is why Gita begins with Arjuna Vishāda Yoga (Arjuna's sorrow). When Devatās (celestial beings) and Dānavās (bad cousins of Devatās) churned the milky ocean (Ksheera Sāgara) for Amrit (ambrosia, the celestial nectar), the first thing that emerged is poison (Hālāhala). When the poison was surrendered to Siva, later only divine nectar came. When we sit for meditation all kinds of bad thoughts come to surface in the mind. When we let them parade and go, the real peace and joy of meditation comes. So is the case in life. Hardships and sorrow are spiritual opportunities for introspection of who we are and the purpose and goal of life.

Equanimity (Sthitaprajnatva):   Gita: 2-55 to 2-72.

Equanimity is a cherished goal in spirituality. In response to Arjuna's question, Krishna explains the need, benefits and qualities of Sthitaprajna (equanimity minded person). These qualities are:

Contentment, humility, detachment, peace, fearlessness, calmness, devoid of anger, equal minded in various situations, sense control, sharp intellect, steadfastness, living in constant integrated awareness of self as a witness, awake when others sleep and sleeps when others are awake (sleeps to worldliness and awake to divinity), witness to happenings, devoid of ego.

Life means ups and downs. When an ECG tracing is flat, it a sign of death. So is life. Ups and downs are part of life and living. Those of us that get attached to body-mind complex (ego) will suffer pain and anguish from these ups and downs. The ones that are anchored to self (Ātman) get non-attached (detached) to body-mind complex (ego) and do not suffer from these normal ups and downs of life. They will be a witness for these happenings. Thus we will be spectators for our own life's drama. We will enjoy our acting; We will enjoy the presence and the role of the director (God) at the same time. This is termed as "constant integrated awareness", "witnessing" and as "Living in Now".

This is the same as Buddhā's Middle Path. After twelve years of fruitless meditation with extremes, he finally realized the Middle Path is the best way to be happy. As long as we see bad as bad and good as good, we are still in the duality of life and not in middle path. Once we start seeing spark of goodness even in bad people and shades of badness (weaknesses) in good people, then we can presume that we are moving towards the middle path.

We need to develop a balanced state of mind to become a Sthitaprajna. When victory and defeat are taken with same still attitude, then one becomes real victor and conqueror of his life. This state is essential for self realization.

Neither seek nor avoid; take what comes. It is liberty to be affected by nothing. Do not merely endure; be unattached.

Swami Vivekananda

40. SALUTATIONS TO FEET (PĀDA NAMASKĀR)

For Hindus, it is a common practice to touch feet of elders, teachers, Gurus, sages and saints. It is done as an act of reverence. Feet (pāda) are the support (Ādhāra) for the body (Ākāra). If we keep going back from disciple to teacher, then to his teacher, to his teacher and it ultimately goes to God as the original and primordial teacher at the very beginning. The salutation to the feet of Guru finally reaches the feet of God the ultimate support of the universe.

Touching feet with forehead signifies surrender (ego). We are in effect saying that I am surrendering my ego at the lotus feet of God, who is the ultimate Ādhāra (support) for all of creation.

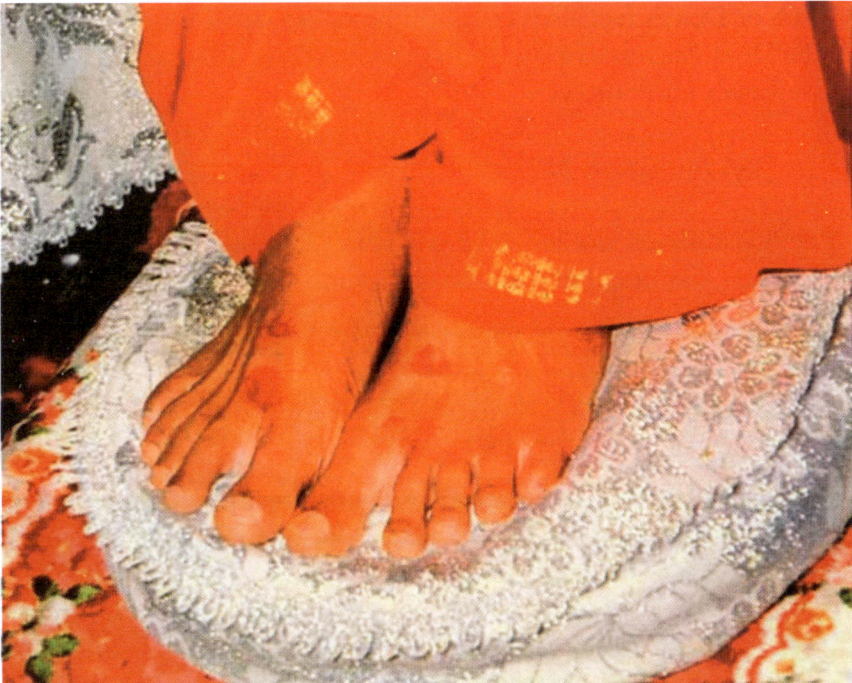

In the words of Bhagawan Sri Sathya Sāi Bāba:

"The purpose of Pādanamaskār is to touch the Feet and have the Sparsan of the Lord. The negative pole (Māyāsakti) and the positive pole (Mahāsakti) have to meet, in order to produce a spiritual current that will flow through you". -- Sathya Sāi Speaks Vol. II. P. 77.

"Further, when opposite poles of two magnets, one huge, the other tiny, come together the small one acquires the power and the nature of the large. The Jivā's head touching the feet of Siva signifies the surrender of his or her ego and merger of Jeevātma and Paramātma. Sacred thoughts enter the mind of a devotee by virtue of the contact with His holy feet. Pādnamaskār virtually means an attitude of surrender to the teacher's instructions and guidance". ----- Necklace of Nine Sai Gems, Vol. VII. P. 35/36.

When we do Pāda Namaskāram to a Guru, the Guru in turn does Pāda Namaskāram to his Guru (mentally). We draw spiritual energy from the Guru's great toes into our forehead (Ājnā Chakra) and the Guru in turn refills thus depleted energy from his Guru, then from the unending source of infinite energy - God.

Guru's or Deity's feet also represent the values stood for by the Guru or the Deity. Surrendering our ego to those values will make us acquire those values into our lives.

"yad bhāvayati tat bhavati"

The Upanishads declare that whatever is thought strongly, that happens., - "as one thinks, so one becomes".

41. MANTRA TANTRA AND YANTRA

The Mantra, Tantra and Yantra take the form of breathing, even without our knowledge as long as we live. "SOHAM" is the mantra. Pranayama is the tantra. Our body is the yantra.

Yantra - Sri Chakra

Mantra:

It is a set of particular words in a particular configuration and rhythm chanted to fulfill a wish. Mantra that is being recited without our knowledge is "Soham". This means that "I am That". I am God only.

Reversing the SOHAM (in Sanskrit) becomes HAMSA.
HAM SA means " Who am I".
SO HAM means " I am that".

Thus our own breath keeps on reminding that we are Atman only.

Tantra:

It means a method (certain procedure) to perform worship in a systemized way. Prānāyāma is the Tantra that describes the method of performing "Soham" Mantra.

Yantra:

It is a geometric figure inscribed (on a metallic plate or paper or others) and is the confluence of the powers of the concerned God. It is the microcosmic representation of macrocosm. Our body is the Yantra for the mantra "Soham". Yantra is a mystical or astronomical diagram or a symbol, said to possess mystical or magical powers.

Symbols in Yantras:

Yantras commonly include squares, triangles, circles and floral patterns.

Lotus:	Represents Chakrās.
Dot:	Represents starting point of creation or the Infinite, Unity, Oneness.
Swastika:	Good luck, prosperity, spiritual victory.
Bija Mantrās:	Acoustic roots in Devanāgari script of Chakrās.
Hexagram (Shatkona):	Balance between upward triangle and Downward triangle.
Circle:	Energy of the element water.
Square:	Energy of the element earth.
Upward Triangle:	Energy of the element fire; energy, Siva.
Downward Triangle:	Energy of the element water; knowledge, Sakti.
Diagonal line:	Energy of the element air.
Horizontal line:	Energy of the element water.
Vertical line:	Energy of the element fire.
Point:	Energy of the element ether

This is the most revered mantra in Hinduism. This comes from a hymn of Rig-Veda attributed to Sage Viswāmitra. He was supposed to have replicated a parallel universe with the strength of Gāyatri Mantra. It is an important part of Upanayana Samskārās for Brahmin men. People of other castes and women are forbidden to chant this mantra. Now there is a reform movement to let everybody including women and other castes to recite Gāyatri Mantra.

Om bhūr bhuvah svah
tát savitúr várenyam
bhárgo devásya dhīmahi
dhíyo yó nah prachodáyāt

The meaning of this Mantra is:

The One that illuminates -

all the three worlds (Bhur, Bhavah and Suvah), the three levels of consciousness (waking, dreaming and deep sleep states), the three aspects of time (past, present and future), the three Gunās (Satwa, Rajo and Tamo Gunas) the three gross, subtle and causal (Stula, sukshma and karana) bodies illuminate my intellect.

It simply says: "I pray to the all pervading Cosmic intelligence – to illuminate my intellect".

43. SPIRITUALITY: RELIGION: CULTURE

These three words, spirituality, religion and culture are intertwined and people commonly get confused. They usually think they are the same. This is not the case. Spirituality deals with spirit, which means distilled essence, or core essence. Religion deals with the travel path towards reaching this essence. Culture on the other hand is the essence of day to day life, living, customs, traditions, clothing, food, family and society that is ingrained as value over a long period of time (history). Examples of these are Indian culture, Arab culture and Western culture.

Spiritual merger into source – River merger into ocean

If religions are the various rivers, spirituality is the ocean they all merge into. The culture is the color, characteristics of the water of these rivers acquired from the soil, where these rivers flow. Once these different rivers merge into ocean, they are left with only with the character of the ocean and nothing else. In each religion there are people who are evolved to a higher level of spirituality. In Hinduism these are called Vedāntins. In Islam they are Sufis. In Christianity lives of Saint Thomas (Gospel of St. Thomas) and Saint Francis of Assisi are examples for this.

While other religions claim exclusivity to the universal truths, Hinduism preaches inclusivity, by saying different religions are different paths to reach the same goal. While this is the ultimate truth, other religions for their own reasons, do not preach or practice this truth. While most other religions practice one level of religion catered to all, Hinduism caters to people at different levels differently depending on their spiritual maturity.

The subject Physics is taught differently to different levels of maturity. In elementary school, it is the basics; in high school and college, it is more and more advanced physics. At university research level the students were allowed free thinking that even permits questioning all the existing principles. Hinduism is the only religion that caters to all the levels, hence called a potential universal religion. That is why Hinduism does not believe in religious conversions. It says that if you are a Christian, be a better Christian. If you are a Muslim, be a better Muslim. If you are a Hindu, be a better Hindu. It promotes in essence brotherhood of mankind and fatherhood of God.

Though culture and religion is inter twined, they are different. Often they are mistaken to be the same. Religion does not talk about clothing, food, habits, customs etc. Culture talks about these subjects. People often confuse religion with culture. Culture is a dynamic evolving process that changes, adapts to the time and place. Religions have some changes when new sages and saints bring in new ways to adapt to the times. Spirituality has no changes, since it is the ultimate truth, good for all times.

44. GOODNESS AND GREATNESS

Hinduism brings a clear distinction between goodness and greatness. In Hinduism humility is upheld as a virtue while in the West, exuberance is a virtue. Often schools and colleges in the West misunderstand this humility exhibited by Hindu children as incompetence.

Goodness is fostered in Hinduism while the West upholds greatness (excellence). Often in order to be great, you have to trample others standing as competition. You have to self-promote (enhancing ego) in order to be recognized as the best. We see this phenomenon in movies and political circles. Goodness on the other hand stems from character and human values. The end-goal of education is character. This splendid character in action is goodness. If character is the flower, goodness is its fragrance. In Rāmāyana Rāvana the villain is more educated than Rāma, and tried to be Great, while Rāma always maintained his goodness. Ultimately Rāma triumphed over Rāvana.

Every action that helps us manifest our divine nature more and more is good; every action that retards it is evil.

Swami Vivekananda

45. INDIVIDUAL (VYASHTI): SOCIETY (SAMASHTI): NATURE (SRISHTI): GOD (PARAMESHTI)

Vyasthi:

Spiritual practice (Sādhana) begins with refining oneself. Then one should serve one's family and make them productive and ethical unit of society.

Samashti:

Next step is to see divinity in the society we live in and do community service as service to God. By doing this we expand ourselves beyond our body's physical limits, beyond the limits of our kith and kin. This is how one develops an attitude of brotherhood of mankind (Vasudhaika Kutumbakam).

Srishti:

Next step in further expansion of one's self, is to see all humans, animals, plants and all elements in nature (earth, water, air, fire and space (Pancha Bhutās) as an aspect of divinity. This means experiencing the Omnipresent Divinity (Eswara Sarva Bhootānam, Eswara Sarva Bhootātmā, Sarva Bhootāntarātmā). Every speck in creation is permeated by Divinity.

Parameshti:

The next natural process is to experience nothing but Divinity. Thus our Third eye gets opened. World becomes a beautiful tapestry of Divinity. We become one with God (Sarvam Brahmam). We get suffused with Ānanda (unending Joy). This is called Moksha, our home.

46. HINDU FESTIVALS

Both Samskārās and festivals in Hinduism are spiritualized personal and community celebrations respectively. All aspects of day to day Hindu life is spiritualized for a higher purpose. While there is large number of festivals celebrated in different parts of India, the following festivals are celebrated on a large scale all over India. A Hindu festival is a spiritualized community celebration.

Some of the Hindu festivals and their significance are:

Ugādi:

Uga (time) + Ādi (beginning) is Ugādi. It is celebrated around March/April marking the beginning of month Chaitra. It is also the spring festival, celebrating the beginning of spring season. It is celebrated as a family gathering with, new clothes, special (Ugādi Patchadi-chutney), made up of ingredients of all tastes (sweet, sour, bitter, salt, tang, hot).

Ugādi Chutney - Ingredients

Ugādi Chutney

This chutney of six tastes consists of:

1. Neem Buds/ Flowers with bitterness, signifying sadness
2. Jaggery for sweetness, signifying happiness
3. Pepper for hot taste, signifying anger
4. Salt for saltiness, signifying fear
5. Tamarind juice for sourness, signifying disgust
6. Unripe Mango for tang, signifying surprise.

People enjoy the Ugādi chutney made with above six tastes so as to welcome life with its variations in the new year. The day ends with listening to the new year's forecast (Panchānga Sravanam).

Sri Rāma Navami:

This is the celebration of birth of Rāma. It is celebrated for nine days commemorating the life story of Rāma in its various stages of life including Sita Rāma Kalyānam and coronation of Rāma. The Sri Rāma Navami festival falls in the ninth waxing day of moon in Chaitram month, which usually falls in March or April.

Rāma

Rāma-Sita-Lakshmana

Rāma with Guha

Guru Purnima:

It is also called Vyāsa Purnima. This was the birth day of sage Veda Vyāsa, the author of Mahā Bhārata, Bhrahma Sutras and 18 Purānās. This day is celebrated on the full moon day of Ashādha, which usually comes in July. This day is used by disciples and devotees to honor their preceptors (Guru).

Rakshā Bandhan:

It is also called Rākhi Purnima. It is celebrated on the full moon day of Srāvana month (Usually comes in August). Rākhi is a special occasion to celebrate the special bond of love between sisters and brothers. On this day sisters tie a Rākhi to the arm of brother, invoke blessing on him.

Rākhi

Rākhi

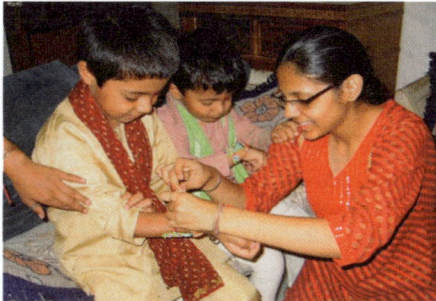

Tying Rākhi

Sri Krishna Janmāshtami:

It is also called Krishna Jayanti, This is the festival celebrating the birth of Lord Sri Krishna. This falls on eighth day of waning moon on Rohini Nakshatra. This usually falls in August or September.

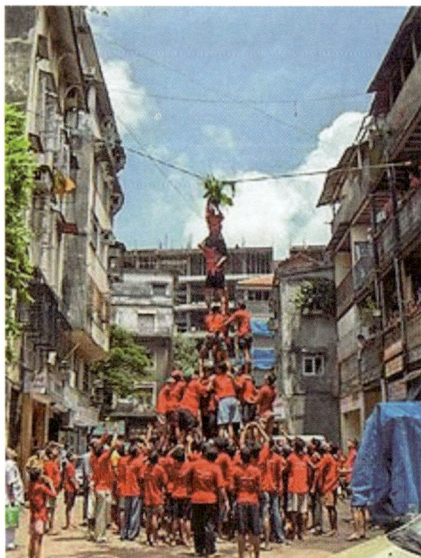

Breaking Dahi Hundi

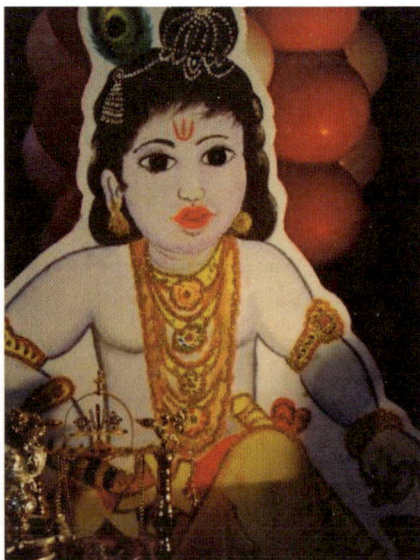

Bala Krishna

Ganesh Chaturthi:

It is a celebration of the birth of Lord Ganesa, son of Siva. It is on the fourth day of the waxing moon of Bhādrapada month. This usually falls in September. Ganesh is considered to represent Mulādhāra Chakra and remover of obstacles. This festival is done for 10 days. On the teenth day a public procession and celebration ends with water immersion of the deity.

Ganesh Water Immersion	Ganesh Celebration	Ganesh Procession

Navarātri:

This is the festival of worship and dance celebrated for nine days. Each day, a special aspect (form) of Sakti is worshipped. This is celebrated on the first nine nights of waxing moon of Aswin month, which usually falls in September or October. This is mainly celebrated in the northeastern part of India.

Navarātri Cultural program

Dasara (Vijaya Dasami):

It is also called Vijaya Dasami or Durgā Puja. This is the celebration of victory of good over the evil, victory of Durga over demon king Mahishāsura, victory of Rāma over Rāvana, Victory of Pāndavās over Kauravās.

Dasara – Durga display

Rāvana effigy Burning

It is celebrated on the tenth day of waxing moon of Aswin month that usually falls in October. This is mostly celebrated in south India on the tenth day of Navāratri.

Deepāvali (Diwāli):

This is also called Diwāli or festival of lights. This festival is celebrated in memory of the occasion of slaying of demon Narakāsura by Lord Krishna and his wife Satya Bhāma. It is also celebrated to mark the return of Rāma and Sita to the kingdom of Ayodhya after fourteen years of exile. This falls on New moon of Aswin month that usually falls in October or November. This is celebrated with lights and fireworks by Hindus all over India and abroad.

Diwāli – Fireworks   Family fire works   Diwāli Lamps

Diwāli Cityscape

Sankrānti (Pongal):

This is also called Pongal and as Makara Sankrānti. It is a winter harvest festival that marks the beginning of the Sun's northward movement from Southern most limits (Uttarāyana). It also represents the Indic solstice when the Sun enters the tenth house of Indian zodiac called Makaram or Capricorn.

Artist Rendering   Sankranthi Floral Designs   Kyte Show

During this festival people decorate their homes with banana and mango leaves. They decorate the floors with designs with calcium powder or rice floor every day for one month culminating on January 14th each year. This festival is to express gratitude to the Sun god for abundant harvest.

Mahā Sivarātri:

It is a festival celebrated every year in reverence of Lord Siva. It literally means the great night of Siva or the night of Siva. It is celebrated every year on the 14th day of the waning moon in Māgha month, which falls usually in February. According to a legend, Pārvati performed Tapas, prayed and meditated on this day to ward off any evil that might befall her husband on the moonless night. Since then, Mahāshivarātri is believed to be an auspicious occasion for a woman to pray for the well-being of her husband and sons.

Lord Siva

Siva Lingam

Another legend is that Siva and Sakti married each other on this day. Yet another legend is when celestials (Devatās) and demons (Dānavās) churned milky ocean for celestial nectar (Amrit), poison (Hālāhala) emerged first. This poison was swallowed by Siva on this day, to protect the world. On this day people do fasting, contemplation and prayers. They maintain all night vigil with Bhajans on Siva.

Holi:

This is a popular, the most colorful spring festival commemorating the slaying of Demoness Holika by Prahlāda (a devotee of Lord Vishnu). This comes on the full moon of the Phālgun month, corresponding to early March. This day is celebrated with spraying of water colors and colored powders on each other.

Holi colors

Spaying Colors

The Vedanta teaches that Nirvana can be attained here and now, that we do not have to wait for death to reach it. Nirvana is the realization of the Self; and after having once known that, if only for an instant, never again can one be deluded by the mirage of personality.

Swami Vivekananda

47. HINDU TEMPLES

At a very personal level Hindus consider their body as the temple of God. They are instructed to take care of the body as if they are taking care of God's abode (Temple). One needs to protect, nourish, clothe, decorate the body as if the one is doing this as a service to the in dwelling soul (Ātma).

The Upanishads declare:

Deho devālaya prokto jivo deva sanātanaha".

This means that, "Body is the temple and the indweller is God".

At a family level, each home has a shrine room with an altar of God. A typical Hindu family performs devotional activities (Puja) in the shrine room after their morning shower. They do some or all sixteen devotional practices (Shodasopachār) as delineated in Chapter 6 in Path of Devotion.

On weekends, holidays, festivals and on special occasions, Hindus visit temples. Hindu temples are places of worship at a community level. They serve as community's religious, cultural, educational and social centers.

Temple constructions are done as per Āgamā Sāstrās (Hindu architectural codes), designed by temple architects (Stapatis) and by sculptors (Silpis). Temples are usually located on river banks, on top of the hills or at other serene locations as per Hindu building code (Vāstu Sāstra). Temple construction includes yoga, astrology and sacred geography (Vāstu).

Four types of Hindu Temples:

There are geographical variations in Hindu temple construction. Most common are four types. They are:

Drāvida type:

These are the temples in South India with tower (Sikhara) consisting of progressively smaller storeys of pavilions that are in pyramidal shape. The smallest pyramid on the top is Stupika as the crowning tower. This type of architecture was transmitted from Pallavas to Cholas in 850-1100 A.D.

Drāvida Type: Sri Venkateswara Temple in Tirumala, Andhra Pradesh, India

Hindu temle, Kualalumpur

Venkateswara temple, Malibu, California, USA

Nāgara type:

These are the temples in North India. Tower (Sikhara) is beehive or curvilinear shaped. The layers of this tower are topped by a large round cushion-like element called 'Amalaka'. The plan is based on a square but the walls are sometimes so segmented, that the tower appears circular in shape This style of temples was believed to have been developed during the 5th century AD. Khajuraho temples in Madhya Pradesh are the most characteristic example of this type of temples.

Nāgara Type: Lakshmana temple in Khajuraho, Madhya Pradesh, India

Vasara type (mixed):

These temples have circular Vimāna and are mainly in Karnataka State and in Southeast Asia. Belur, Halebidu and Somanāthpura. The Chālukyas built them around 500-753 AD. They are the typical examples of this type of temples.

Vasara type temple at Ankor Wat in Cambodia

Kalinga type:

These temples are a sub type of Nāgara temple of north India. They are located in Orissa and northern Andhra Pradesh states of India. Most popular of this type are the Lingarāja temple at Bhuvaneswar (11th century A.D), Jagannāth temple at Puri (12th century A.D) and Sun temple at Konark (13th century A.D). In this style of temple, the Vimāna is constructed on square base and has a curvilinear tower (Sikhara). These horizontal rectangular platforms are arranged in progressively receding formation to constitute a pyramidal superstructure.

Kalinga type temple: Puri Jagannath Temple, Orissa state, India

Parts of temple and their representation:

Temples are the microcosmic representation of the macrocosmic universe. They represent the body of Divinity. They represent the seven energy centers (Chakrās). A temple typically has five, three or one layers (Prākārās).

Rājagopuram:

Most big Hindu temples have five layers (Prākārās). Most USA Hindu temples have three layers (Prākārās). The five layers represent five sheaths (Pancha Kosās) in humans. Three layers represent three bodies, gross (Sthula), subtle (Sukshma) and causal (Kārana) bodies. One layered temple represents causal body (Ānandmaya kosa).

The entry way to the temple represents feet of God. This is 3, 5, 7 or 9 stories tall in height depending on the height of statue of the deity. This represents the gross body. All the images and drawings on the Rājagopuram represent the gross body.

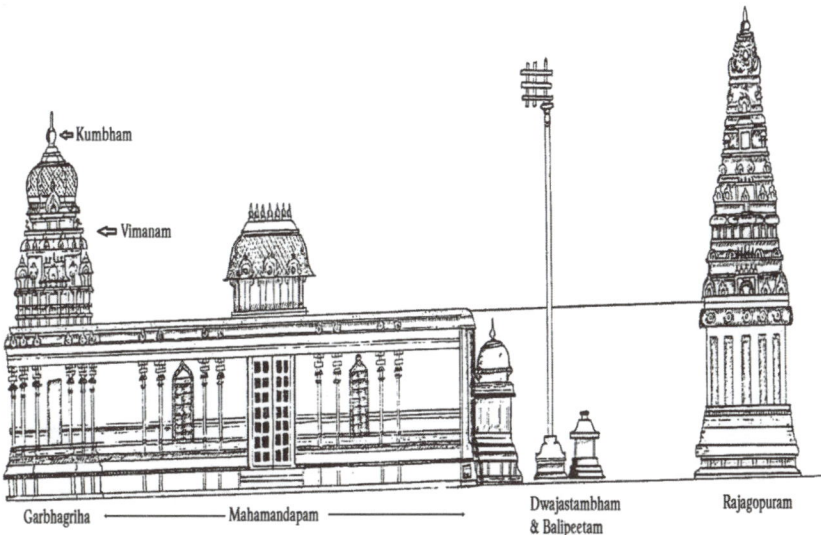

Parts of Hindu Temple

Balipeetham (Sacrifice Rock):

In the olden days people used to offer sacrifices at this stone. This is located between Rājagopuram and Dhwajasthambham. Balipetam is the place we need to sacrifice our animal tendencies (Arishadvargās) and ego, before we enter the inner sanctum of the temple.

Dhwajasthambham:

This is the flag pole of the temple. It has the vehicle (Vāhana) of the deity, Bull (Nandi) in Siva temples and eagle (Garuda) in Vaishnava temples. This is up to a maximum of 42 feet in height, depending on the height of the statue of the Deity.

Garbhagriham:

This is the Sanctum Santorum of the temple. This represents heart (Anāhata chakra) of the deity. This is where Paramātman was installed as a statue for worship.

Ardhamandapam or Mahāmandapam:

This is the open covered area in front of Garbhagriham. This is where people rest for awhile after visiting the deity. Most Pujas and Bhajans and mini cultural programs take place here. However, major cultural programs are done in the adjacent cultural hall.

Vimānam or Sikhara:

This is the structure above the Garbhagriha. This is considered to be Visuddha and Ajnā Chakras.

Kalasa:

This is the metal vessel above the Vimāna. This represents Sahasrāra Chakra and represents top of the head of Deity.

Pushkarini or Kalyāni (Temple Tank):

This is the open water tank next to the temple for devotees to take bath before entering the temple.

Kumbhābhishekam:

Once every twelve years, the spiritual energy is recharged by doing sacred water-bathing ceremony (Abhisheka) to the Kalasa on the Vimānam. This is called Kumbhābhishekam. Similar recharging for holy rivers is done every twelve years. This is called Pushkara or Kumbhamela.

Mulādhāra, Swādhishtana and Manipuraka Chakrās are underground below the Garbhagriha. Temples are built on a mandala with 64 or 81 squares. Most temples are built with deity facing east.

Pradakshina:

After entering into the temple through the Rājagopurm entrance, devotees do clockwise circumambulation three times, each time prostrating at the Balipeetham as a gesture of sacrifice of ego.

Ātma Pradakshina:

After visiting the Garbhagriha devotees do self circambulation (Ātma Pradakshina), symbolizing the surrender of body mind complex (Ego) to Ātma inside the body.

48. HINDU PRIESTS AND PREACHERS

Hindu priests perform Vedic rituals as mentioned in the sixteen Samskārās earlier in chapter 18. They also perform devotional rituals (Pujās) and Homams in the temples. While most priests are Brahmins by birth, recently people of other castes are also being trained to take this role. Priests limit themselves to the ritualistic aspect of Hindu religion and do not preach as is seen in other religions.

Hindu Priest performing temple ritual   Swami Chinmayananda

A preacher is the one who is a self-realized soul that can transmit his personal experience to others. These include several Gurus, Sages, Saints, Yogis and Yoginis. Their preachings transform large mass of people into spirituality. This is usually done in the Āsrams (hermitages) of the sages and Gurus.

49. HINDU SCRIPTURES

Sruti Literature: (heard by sages and saints as divine revelation)

1. **Vedās:** Rig Veda, Yajur Veda, Sāma Veda and Atharvana Veda.

   (Samhita, Brāhmana, Aranyaka and Upanishad)

   Upanishads: (11 Mukhya Upanishads)

1.	Aitareya Upanishad	- Rig Veda
2.	Taittiriya Upanishad	- Krishna Yajur Veda
3.	Katha Upanishad	- Krishna Yajur Veda
4.	Svetāsvatar Upanishad	- Krishna Yajur Veda
5.	Brihadāranyaka Upanishad	- Sukla Yajur Veda
6.	Isa Upanishad	- Sukla Yajur Veda
7.	Chhandogya Upanishad	- Sāma Veda
8.	Kena Upanishad	- Sāma Veda
9.	Prasna Upanishad	- Atharvana Veda
10.	Māndukya Upanishad	- Atharvana Veda
11.	Mundaka Upanishad	- Atharvana Veda

Smriti Literature: (written in script and transmitted)

1. **Smritis:** Manu Smriti, Gautama Smriti, Yājnavalkya Smriti.

2. **Vedāngās:** Siksha (phonetics), Vyākarana (grammar), Chandas(meter), Nirukta (etymology), Jyotisha (astronomy), Kalpa (ritual).

3. **Darsanās:** Nyaya, Vaiseshika, Sāmkhya, Yoga, Purva Mimāmsa, Uttara Mimāmsa **(Brahma Sutras)**

4. **Ithihāsa: Rāmāyana, Mahābhārata (Bhagavad-Gita)**

5. **Purānās:** Agni, **Bhāgavata**, Bhavishya, Brahma, Brahmānda, Garuda, Brahmavaivarta, Kurma, Linga, Mārkandeya, Matsya, Nārada, Padma, Skāndha, Vāmana, Varāha, Vāyu, Vishnu.
   (18 major Puranas)

6. **Upavedās:** These are the treatises with subject material of additional sciences added to the Vedas

Ayur Veda	added to Atharvana Veda (Medicine)
Artha Sāstra:	added to Rig Veda (Polity & Economy)
Dhanur Veda:	added to Yajur Veda (Archery)
Gāndharvaveda:	added to Sama Veda (Bharata Nātya, Kāma Sutra)
Stapatya Veda	added to Adharvana Veda (Vāstu Sāstra)

7. **Tantras:** Mantrās, Yantrās, Mandalās, Cosmograms, Mudrās, Kundalini Power, Sexo Yogic Exercises, Bandhās.

8. **Āgamās:** Vaishnava Āgamās (Vishnu Samhita), Saiva Āgamās, Sākteya Āgamās

9. **Upangās:** Logical & Ritualistic forms of thought.

10. **Siddhantās:** Dwaita, Visishtādwaita, Adwaita.

Prasthānatraya: (Three great Scriptures)
Bhagavad-Gita,
Upanishads,
Brahma Sutras.

Together, they are called Prasthāna Traya.

50. SPIRITUALITY DEFINED FOR THE DISINTERESTED

There are some who get frightened or turned off at words of spirituality and religion. For these people, I summarized the essence of spirituality into six do's, six don'ts. If this 6+6 is difficult, follow three. If three are difficult follow two. If two are difficult, follow atleast one.

A.   Six do's and six don'ts:

Six **GOOD** things to practice:

1.	Satya:	Truth
2.	Dharma:	Right Conduct
3.	Sānti:	Peace
4.	Prema:	Love
5.	Ahimsa:	Non-Violence
6.	Tyāga	Sacrifice of ego

Six **BAD** things (Arishadvargās) to get rid of:

1.	Kāma:	Desire
2.	Krodha:	Anger
3.	Lobha:	Miserliness
4.	Moha:	Delusion
5.	Mada:	Ego
6.	Mātsarya	Envy

B. Be Positive: Three things to follow:

Think, See and Hear Good
Speak Good
Do Good

(Any thing that unites is good and any thing that divides is bad)

C. Two dictums to follow: Two things to follow:

1. "Love All – Serve All" - Sathya Sāi Bāba
Intense Love for God is Bhakti. Seeing God in All is Jnāna.

Combined together "Love All" constitutes Bhakti + Jnāna Yoga.

Serving All is Karma Yoga.
All three yogas (Bhakti + Jnāna + Karma) combined together in practice is:

"Love All – Serve All".

2. "Help Ever – Hurt Never" – Sathya Sāi Bāba

"Ashtādasa purāneshu
vyasena vachanam dwayam,
paropakarah punayāya
pāpāya parapedanam"

This means that the essence of the eighteen puranas as Vyāsa said is helping others is virtue (punyam) and hurting others is sinful (pāpam). Helping always and hurting never.

Helping is Daiva Sampatti (qualities of Divinity). Hurting is Dānava Sampatti (quality of demons). From being Mānava (human being) we should ascend up the ladder to aquire and practice Daivik (Godly) qualities. We should not deteriate to become danavas (demons) by hurting others (Asurik quality). Hence practice:

"Help Ever – Hurt Never".

D. Attitude of Gratitude:

One thing at least to follow:

The essence of all of spirituality in one sentence is an attitude of gratitude. We should be grateful to air, water, fire, Earth, Ākāsa, parents, teachers, friends, spouse, sunrise, sunsets, moon shine, cool breeze and for life and living. It is moving from an attitude of entitlement to attitude of gratitude. It is an acknowledgement of all pervading Divinity and its hand in all aspects of our life. Giving back always more than one receives is an expression of that gratitude.

51. SPIRITUALITY DEMYSTIFIED: EIGHT STEPS TO HAPPINESS

Faith – Effort – Acceptance – Adjustment – Forgiveness– Savoring –Equanimity – Gratitude

1.   Faith:

Faith is the firm, unwavering belief that there is a cosmic intelligence, cosmic energy and cosmic sustenance at work for all the events that happen in the cosmos, this world and in our life. This belief is called Bhakti.

This initial blind faith based on advice of parents, friends and society, later grows and establishes firmly. Pretty soon this blossoms into a direct experience of the unseen divine hand at work. This direct experience confirms and validates the blind faith. This is the spiritual foundation on which the mansion of spirituality is built.

2.   Effort:

Human effort is mandatory at all times. Best planning with available information and best effort with all our energies is a must in practicing spirituality. Spirituality is never laziness as some people mistakenly think. "As you sow, so shall you reap". Spare no efforts. Put 110% of effort. After following the first and second step, follow the third step, which is equally important.

3.   Acceptance:

Without acceptance of the results, we become frustrated some times when our intense effort does not produce the desired results.   Intense effort without acceptance brings in pain and suffering. Acceptance before effort brings in laziness. We have control only on the planning and effort. We absolutely have no control on the results. Accepting gracefully the results, makes it a Nishkāma Karma and elevates us spiritually.

4.   Adjustment:

We should be continuous learners in life. When we cease learning, it is equivalent to death. All experiences, both good and bad are great teachers. We should have open mind to learn from experiences and continually improve. This process is called adjustment. This is spontaneous in nature. All living beings adapt and adjust for survival and future growth and development. Rigid ones are the ones that break first. Flexible ones grow further.

5.   Forgiveness:

Forgiveness shows our intention to be porous, where we respect others and make room for them in our hearts. This expansion of ourselves is to include others in our being. This is spiritual progress. Hurtful acts of others, should not make us judge them harshly. Instead it should help us introspect ourselves, whether we have ever committed such hurtful acts towards others. If this analysis (introspection) reveals the fact that we have committed similar mistakes, we should make immediate effort to correct ourselves. This process will help us grow spiritually. Forgiving is true giving up of our ego. Ego sublimation is the ultimate frontier of spirituality.

6.   Savoring:

Savoring is an expression of experience of omnipresent Divinity. Be happy. Enjoy every moment as a gift like a child. We take life for granted and lead a life of indifference and unawareness. Let us bring awareness to life. Let us bring presence to life. This is called living in "now" Forgetting life brings misery and sorrow. Awareness of true presence of life drives away misery and suffering and brings in joy and happiness in its place.

"Don't Worry – Be Happy".

7.   Equanimity:

Vedānta calls this Sthitaprajna state as discussed earlier in Chapter 39. This is also same as Buddhā's middle path. We tend to see the world as black and white. As long we see the world this way, we see a world of cruelty, misery and sorrow. World is a mirror in front of us. We see ourselves in the world. If we are miserable in side, we see a miserable world outside. If we are happy inside we see a happy world outside.

In order to improve the world outside, we need to improve ourselves inside. As long as we see extremes, we are not balanced. As we grow in spirituality, we start seeing the different shades of grey in between black and white. This means that we have started seeing goodness in other people and faults in ourselves to improve. Pretty soon we develop a balanced mind, a still mind, a equanimous mind suitable for self realization (Moksha).

8.   Gratitude:

It is the hall mark of spirituality. We spend life with an attitude of entitlement when our ego is strong and thick. As we advance in spirituality our ego start melting and we become more mellow and humble. With this humility comes the attitude of gratitude. This shows our porosity and transparency. Through this transparency (purity of heart) we will have the experience of Divinity (Moksha).

Tears of gratitude should flow down when we smell the fragrance of a flower, when cool breeze touches our check, when we see a beautiful sunset, when we think about parents, spouse, children, grand children, in fact everything and anything. This means that we are experiencing the omnipresent Divinity. Our vision has transformed. Our third eye (inner vision) has opened and burnt the attitude of entitlement and with it our ego.

We should feel free to express this gratitude in thoughts, words and deeds at every opportunity that we get. Our lives get sanctified, our life's journey becomes a pilgrimage and our world becomes a holy place to live.

It is our own mental attitude which makes the world what it is for us. Our thought make things beautiful, our thoughts make ugly. The whole world is in our own minds. Learn to see things in the proper light. First, believe in this world -- that there is meaning behind everything. Everything in the world is good, is holy and beautiful. If you see something evil, think that you are not understanding it in the right light. Throw the burden on yourselves.

Swami Vivekananda

52. QUOTES OF DISTINGUISHED WESTERN SCHOLARS ON HINDUISM

1. India is the cradle of the human race, the birthplace of human speech, the mother of history, the grandmother of legend, and the great grandmother of tradition. Our most valuable and most instructive materials in the history of man are treasured up in India only. --- **Mark Twain, American author.**

2. India was the motherland of our race, and Sanskrit the mother of Europe's languages: she was the mother of our philosophy; mother, through the Arabs, of much of our mathematics; mother, through the Buddha, of the ideals embodied in Christianity; mother, through the village community, of self-government and democracy. Mother India is in many ways the mother of us all. --- **Will Durant, American historian**

3. We owe a lot to the Indians, who taught us how to count, without which no worthwhile scientific discovery could have been made. --- **Albert Einstein.**

4. If I were asked under what sky the human mind has most fully developed some of its choicest gifts, has most deeply pondered on the greatest problems of life, and has found solutions, I should point to India. --- **Max Mueller, German scholar**

5. If there is one place on the face of earth where all the dreams of living men have found a home from the very earliest days when man began the dream of existence, it is India.
   --- **Romain Rolland, French scholar**

6.	Whenever I have read any part of the Vedas, I have felt that some unearthly and unknown light illuminated me. In the great teaching of the Vedas, there is no touch of sectarianism. It is of all ages, climes, and nationalities and is the royal road for the attainment of the Great Knowledge. When I read it, I feel that I am under the spangled heavens of a summer night. --- **Henry David Thoreau, American Thinker & Author**

7.	In the great books of India, an empire spoke to us, nothing small or unworthy, but large, serene, consistent, the voice of an old intelligence, which in another age and climate had pondered and thus disposed of the questions that exercise us. --- **R.W. Emerson, American Author**

8.	There are some parts of the world that, once visited, get into your heart and won't go. For me, India is such a place. When I first visited, I was stunned by the richness of the land, by its lush beauty and exotic architecture, by its ability to overload the senses with the pure, concentrated intensity of its colors, smells, tastes, and sounds... I had been seeing the world in black & white and, when brought face-to-face with India, experienced everything re-rendered in brilliant Technicolor".
	--- **Keith Bellows, National Geographic Society**

9.	India conquered and dominated China culturally for 20 centuries without ever having to send a single soldier across her border.
	--- **Hu Shih, former Ambassador of China to USA**

10.	So far as I am able to judge, nothing has been left undone, either by man or nature, to make India the most extraordinary country that the sun visits on his rounds. Nothing seems to have been forgotten, nothing overlooked. --- **Mark Twain**

11.	India will teach us the tolerance and gentleness of mature mind, understanding spirit and a unifying, pacifying love for all human beings. --- **Will Durant, American Historian**

12. From the Vedas we learn a practical art of surgery, medicine, music, house building under which mechanized art is included. They are encyclopedia of every aspect of life, culture, religion, science, ethics, law, cosmology and meteorology.
--- **William James, American Author**

13. There is no book in the world that is so thrilling, stirring and inspiring as the Upanishads. ('Sacred Books of the East')
--- **Max Mueller, German Scholar**

14. It is already becoming clear that a chapter which had a Western beginning will have to have an Indian ending if it is not to end in the self-destruction of the human race. At this supremely dangerous moment in history, the only way of salvation for mankind is the Indian way. --- **Dr. Arnold Toynbee**

15. The Sanskrit language, whatever be its antiquity is of wonderful structure, more perfect than the Greek, more copious than the Latin and more exquisitely refined than either.
--- **Sir William Jones, British Orientalist**

16. Gravitation was known to the Hindus (Indians) before the birth of Newton. The system of blood circulation was discovered by them centuries before Harvey was heard of. --- **P. Johnstone**

17. They were very advanced Hindu astronomers in 6000 BC. Vedas contain an account of the dimension of Earth, Sun, Moon, Planets and Galaxies." ('Calendars and Constellation)
--- **Emmelin Plunret**

18. She (India) has left indelible imprints on one fourth of the human race in the course of a long succession of centuries. She has the right to reclaim ... her place amongst the great nations summarizing and symbolizing the spirit of humanity. From Persia to the Chinese sea, from the icy regions of Siberia to Islands of Java and Borneo, India has propagated her beliefs, her tales, and her civilization. --- **Sylvia Levi**

19. India has two million gods, and worships them all. In religion all other countries are paupers; India is the only millionaire. --- **Mark Twain**

20. Where can we look for sages like those whose systems of philosophy were prototypes of those of Greece: to whose works Plato, Thales and Pythagoras were disciples? Where do I find astronomers whose knowledge of planetary systems yet excites wonder in Europe as well as the architects and sculptors whose works claim our admiration, and the musicians who could make the mind oscillate from joy to sorrow, from tears to smile with the change of modes and varied intonation?--- **Colonel James Todd**

21. There has been no more revolutionary contribution than the one which the Hindus (Indians) made when they invented ZERO. ('Mathematics for the Millions') --- **Lancelot Hogben**

22. India - The land of Vedas, the remarkable works contain not only religious ideas for a perfect life, but also facts which science has proved true. Electricity, radium, electronics, airship, all were known to the seers who founded the Vedas. ---**Wheeler Wilcox**

23. After the conversations about Indian philosophy, some of the ideas of Quantum Physics that had seemed so crazy suddenly made much more sense. --- **W.Heisenberg, German Physicist**

24. The surgery of the ancient Indian physicians was bold and skilful. A special branch of surgery was dedicated to rhinoplasty or operations for improving deformed ears, noses and forming new ones, which European surgeons have now borrowed. --- **Sir W. Hunter, British Surgeon**

25. An examination of Indian Vedic doctrines shows that it is in tune with the most advanced scientific and philosophical thought of the West. --- **Sir John Woodroffe**

26. Our present knowledge of the nervous system fits in so accurately with the internal description of the human body given in the Vedas (5000 years ago). Then the question arises whether the Vedas are really religious books or books on anatomy of the nervous system and medicine. ('The Vedic Gods') --- **B.G. Rele**

27. One Billion-Year-Old fossil prove life began in India: AFP Washington reports in Science Magazine that German Scientist Adolf Seilachar and Indian Scientist P.K. Bose have unearthed fossil in Churhat a town in Madhya Pradesh, India which is 1.1 billion years old and has rolled back the evolutionary clock by more than 500 million years. --- **Adolf Seilachar & P.K. Bose, Scientists**

28. Vedas are the most rewarding and the most elevating books which can be possible in the world. (Works VI p.427). --- **Schopenhauer**

53. QUOTES FROM DISTINGUISHED PEOPLE ON BHAGAVAD GITA

1. From a clear knowledge of the Bhagavad-Gita all the goals of human existence become fulfilled. Bhagavad Gita is the manifest quintessence of all the teachings of the Vedic scriptures.
    - Ādi Sankarāchārya.

2. When I read the Bhagavad-Gita and reflect about how God created this universe everything else seems so superfluous.
    - Albert Einstein.

3. I have made the Bhagavad-Gita as the main source of my inspiration and guide for the purpose of scientific investigations and formation of my theories.
    - Albert Einstein.

4. The Bhagavad-Gita has a profound influence on the spirit of mankind by its devotion to God which is manifested by actions.
    - Dr. Albert Schweitzer.

5. The Bhagavad-Gita is the most systematic statement of spiritual evolution of endowing value to mankind. It is one of the most clear and comprehensive summaries of perennial philosophy ever revealed; hence its enduring value is subject not only to India but to all of humanity.
    - Aldus Huxley.

6. The idea that man is like unto an inverted tree seems to have been current in by-gone ages. The link with Vedic conceptions is provided by Plato in his Timaeus in which it states..."behold we are not an earthly but a heavenly plant." This correlation can be discerned by what Krishna expresses in chapter 15 of Bhagavad-Gita.
   - Carl Jung.

7. In the morning I bathe my intellect in the stupendous and cosmogonal philosophy of the Bhagavad-Gita, in comparison with which our modern world and its literature seems puny and trivial.
   - Henry David Thoreau.

8. I would say to the readers of the Scriptures, if they wish for a good book, read the Bhagavad-Gita .... translated by Charles Wilkins. It deserves to be read with reverence even by Yankees.... "Besides the Bhagavad-Gita, our Shakespeare seems sometimes youthfully green... Ex oriente lux may still be the motto of scholars, for the Western world has not yet derived from the East all the light it is destined to derive thence.
   - Henry David Thoreau.

9. The marvel of the Bhagavad-Gita is its truly beautiful revelation of life's wisdom which enables philosophy to blossom into religion
   - Herman Hesse.

10. The Bhagavad-Gita deals essentially with the spiritual foundation of human existence. It is a call of action to meet the obligations and duties of life; yet keeping in view the spiritual nature and grander purpose of the universe.
    - Jawaharlal Nehru.

11. The Bhagavad-Gita calls on humanity to dedicate body, mind and soul to pure duty and not to become mental voluptuaries at the mercy of random desires and undisciplined impulses.
    - Mahatma Gandhi.

12. When doubts haunt me, when disappointments stare me in the face, and I see not one ray of hope on the horizon, I turn to Bhagavad-Gita and find a verse to comfort me; and I immediately begin to smile in the midst of overwhelming sorrow. Those who meditate on the Gita will derive fresh joy and new meanings from it every day.
   - Mahatma Gandhi.

13. Yoga has two different meanings - a general meaning and a technical meaning. The general meaning is the joining together or union of any two or more things. The technical meaning is a state of stability and peace and the means or practices which lead to that state. The Bhagavad-Gita uses the word with both meanings. Lord Krishna is real Yogi who can maintain a peaceful mind in the midst of any crisis.
   - Mata Amritanandamayi Devi.

14. Maharishi calls the Bhagavad-Gita the essence of Vedic Literature and a complete guide to practical life. It provides all that is needed to raise the consciousness of man to the highest possible level. Maharishi reveals the deep, universal truths of life that speak to the needs and aspirations of everyone.
   - Maharshi Mahesh Yogi

15. The Bhagavad-Gita is where God Himself talks to His devotee Arjuna.
   - Paramahansa Yogananda.

16. I can say that in the Bhagavad-Gita As It Is I have found explanations and answers to questions I had always posed regarding the interpretations of this sacred work, whose spiritual discipline I greatly admire. If the asceticism and ideal of the apostles which form the message of the Bhagavad-Gita As It Is were more widespread and more respected, the world in which we live would be transformed into a better, more fraternal place.
   - Dr. Paul Lesourd.

17. I owed a magnificent day to the Bhagavad-Gita. It was the first of books; it was as if an empire spoke to us, nothing small or unworthy, but large, serene, consistent, the voice of an old intelligence which in another age and climate had pondered and thus disposed of the same questions which exercise us.
- **Ralph Waldo Emerson.**

18. The Bhagavad-Gita is an empire of thought and in its philosophical teachings Krishna has all the attributes of the full-fledged monotheistic deity and at the same time the attributes of the Upanishadic absolute.
- **Ralph Waldo Emerson.**

19. In order to approach a creation as sublime as the Bhagavad-Gita with full understanding it is necessary to attune our soul to it.
- **Rudolph Steiner.**

20. Though everything else is taken away from him, though he has to walk the streets, cold, hungry and alone, though he may know no human being into whose eyes he can look and find understanding, he shall yet be able to go his way with a smile on his lips, for he has gained inward freedom
- **Sarvepalli Radhakrishnan.** (philosopher and political leader)

21. Seek that Divine Knowledge by knowing which nothing remains to be known!' For such a person knowledge and ignorance has only one meaning: Have you knowledge of God? If yes, you are a jnani. If not, you are ignorant. As said in the Gita, chapter XIII/11, knowledge of Self, observing everywhere the object of true Knowledge i.e. God, all this is declared to be true Knowledge (wisdom); what is contrary to this is ignorance.
- **Sri Ramakrishna**

22. The Bhagavad-Gita is a true scripture of the human race a living creation rather than a book, with a new message for every age and a new meaning for every civilization.
- **Sri Aurobindo.**

23. Science describes the structures and processes; philosophy attempts at their explanation.----- When such a perfect combination of both science and philosophy is sung to perfection that Krishna was, we have in this piece of work an appeal both to the head and heart.
- **Swami Chinmayanand.**

24. Nothing has ever arisen in my life, internal or external, that the Gita has not made clear and enabled me to deal with or understand.
- **Swami Nirmalananda Giri.**

25. The secret of karma yoga which is to perform actions without any fruitive desires is taught by Lord Krishna in the Bhagavad-Gita.
- **Swami Vivekananda.**

26. Karma, Bhakti, and Jnana are but three paths to this end. And common to all the three is renunciation. Renounce the desires, even of going to heaven, for every desire related with body and mind creates bondage. Our focus of action is neither to save the humanity nor to engage in social reforms, not to seek personal gains, but to realize the indwelling Self itself.
- **Swami Vivekananda.**

27. I read the Indian poem for the first time when I was in my country estate in Silesia and, while doing so, I felt a sense of overwhelming gratitude to God for having let me live to be acquainted with this work. It must be the most profound and sublime thing to be found in the world.
- **Wlhielm von Humboldt (1767- 1835)**

54. RECOMMENDED READING

1. "The Complete Works of Swami Vivekananda", Vol. 1-9, Distributed by Vedanta Press, Hollywood, CA 90068.

2. "The Gospel of Sri Ramakrishna" Sri Ramakrishna Math, Madras 600004, India

3. "The Holy Gita" commentary by Swami Chinmayananda, Chinmaya Mission trust, Bombay – 400072, India.

4. "Gita Makarandamu" by Sri Vidya Praksananda Giri Swamy, Sri Suka Brahma Asramam, Sri Kalahasti, AP, India (Telugu).

5. "Sathya Sai Speaks" by Bhagawan Sri Satya Sai Baba, Vol. 1-42, Sathya Sai Book Center of America, Tustin, CA 92780.

6. "Vahini Series" (Bhagavata, Dharma, Dhyana, Gita, Jnana, Leela Kaivalya, Prashanthi, Prasnothara. Prema, Rama Katha Rasa, Sandeha Nivarini, Sathya Sai, Sutra, Upanishad and Vidya Vahini) and Sathyopanishad by Bhagavan Sri Sathya Sai Baba, Sathya Sai Book Center of America, Tustin, CA 92780.

7. "Summer Showers in Brindavan" Series 1-12 (1972-2002), by Bhagavan Sri Sathya Sai Baba, Sathya Sai Book Center of America, Tustin, CA 92780.

8. "Narada's way of Divine Love" (Narada Bhakti Sutras), Translation with commentary by Swami Prabhavananda, Sri Ramakrishna Math, Madras 600004, India.

9. "The Essentials of Hinduism" by Swami Bhaskarananda, Vedanta Society of western Washington, Seattle, WA 98102.

10. "Am I A Hindu" by Ed. Viswanathan, Halo Books, Palm Desert, CA 92260.

11. "The Book of Yoga", by Lucy Lidell, The Sivananda Yoga Centre, Ebury Press.

12. " BKS Iyengar Light on Yoga" by B. K. S. Iyengar, Unwin Paperbacks.

13. "The Vedas" by Sri Chandrasekharendra Saraswati, Bharatiya Vidya Bhavan,.

14. "Mananam Publication Series" by Chinmaya Mission West, Los Altos, CA

15. "Hinduism Today" 107 Kaholalele Road, Kapaa, HI 96746-9304, USA.

16. The Secret Teachings of the Vedas, Stephen Knapp.

17. The Heart of Hinduism, Stephen Knapp.

55. GLOSSARY OF HINDUISM TERMS

Ādi Sakti: Form of cosmic energy. Feminine aspect of divinity.

Ādi Sankara: The first Hindu philosopher who consolidated the principles of the Advaita (non-dualism) Vedānta philosophy.

Adharma: Opposite of Dharma - un-righteousness.

Advaita Vedānta: A school of Hindu philosophy often called a monistic or non-dualistic system which refers to the indivisibility (non distinct) of the Self (Ātman) from the Whole (Brahman).

Adhyātmic: Spiritual. Towards spirituality.

Āgāmi Karma: Action done in this life that will produce results in later lives.

Agni: The sacred Hindu fire God.

Ahamkāra: A Sanskrit term that refers to the ego of one's self, the identification of one's own ego (body-mind complex).

Ahimsā: A religious concept which advocates non-violence and a respect for all life. Gandhi promoted this concept.

Amrit: Ambrosia, the food of the Gods, which makes the partaker immortal.

Ānanda: Unending happiness or bliss.

Āranyaka: Part of the Hindu Śrutis that discuss philosophy and sacrifice.

Arjuna: The third of Pāndavās and Krishnā's cousin. His doubts on the battle field led to Krishna expounding the Gita.

Artha: Wealth, one of the objects of human life, the others being Dharma, (righteous- ness), Kāma (satisfaction of desires), Moksha (spiritual salvation).

Ardha Nāreeswara: Siva in the form of half man (Siva) and half woman (Pārvati).

Ātma: The underlying metaphysical self, sometimes translated as spirit or soul.

Avatār: Incarnation of God in human form like Rāma, Krishna.

Ayodhyā: Capital of Rāma's kingdom. The city in the country of Kosala.

Balarāma: Elder brother of Lord Krishna.

Balarāma: An Avatār or incarnation of Ādisesha the thousand-hooded serpent on which Lord Vishnu (protector aspect of trinity) reclines in Vaikuntha (abode of Vishnu).

Bālya: Childhood.

Bhagawān: Form of address to Gods and great rishis, example-Bhagawān Sri Krishna, Nārada, Vyāsa. A Sanskrit word meaning "Holy or Blessed one". It is a title of veneration, often translated as "Lord" and refers to God.

Bhagavad-Gita: The national gospel contained in Mahābhārata, Part of the epic poem Mahābhārata, located in the Bhishma–Parva chapters 23–40. A core sacred text of Hinduism and philosophy.

Bhajan: A Hindu devotional song. Great importance is attributed to the singing of bhajans within the Bhakti movement.

Bhaktī: A Sanskrit term that means intense love for God. This devotion is expressed by action (service). A person who practices bhakti is called bhakta.

Bhaktī Yoga: The Hindu term for the spiritual practice of fostering of loving devotion to God, called bhakti.

Bharata: Means "to be or being maintained"). Bharat may be 1. a name of Agni 2. a name of Rudra 3. one of the Ādityās 4. Emperor Bharata, son of Dushyanta and Sakuntalā 5. Bharata (Rāmāyana), a son of Dasaratha, younger brother of Rāma 6. Bharata Muni, the author of the Natyasāstra 7. Bharata (Bhāgavata), the eldest of a hundred sons of a saintly king by name Rishabha Deva according to the Bhāgavata Purāna.

Bhārata: Meaning ("descended from Bharata"). Bhārata may refer to 1. The Bhāratās, an Āryan tribe of the Rig-Veda 2. an early epic forming the core of the Mahābhārata (allegedly comprising about a quarter of the extended epic) 3. the Republic of India.

Bhīshma: Bhīshma was son of Santanu, the great Knight and guardian of the imperial house of Kurus.

Brahmā: Creator of the universe, The Hindu creator god, and one of the Trimurti (Trinity), the others being Vishnu and Siva. He must not be confused with the Supreme Cosmic Spirit of Hindu philosophy Brahman.

Brahmacharya: Celibacy, chastity; the stage of life of Vedic study in which chastity and service are essential, The word Brahmacharya symbolizes a person who is leading a life in quest of Brahma, or in other words a Hindu student.

Brahman: The name given to the concept of the unchanging, infinite, immanent and transcendent reality, which is the Divine Ground of all being.

Brāhmin: One of four fundamental group of Hindu caste system symbolically attributed to color (Varna), consisting of scholars, priests and spiritual teachers. Self realized person.

Braj: Braj (also known as Brij or Brajbhoomi) is a region in Uttar Pradesh of India, around Mathura-Vrindāvan. It is considered to be the land of Krishna and is derived from the Sanskrit word Vraja.

Brindāvan: A town on the site of an ancient forest which is the region where Lord Krishna spent his childhood days. It lies in the Braj region.

Buddha: Saint Gautam Buddha who founded Buddhism.

Caste: Portuguese word to describe in a Western context the Hindu system of classification of people (Jāti).

Chakra: An energy node in the human body. The seven main chakras are described as being aligned in an ascending column from the base of the spine to the top of the head. Each Chakra is associated with a certain color, multiple specific functions, an aspect of consciousness, a classical element, with other distinguishing characteristics.

Chitta: Discriminating mind.

Chitta Suddhi: Purity of heart. Unison of thoughts, words and actions. Also called Trikarana Suddhi.

Daityās: The Demons. Daityās are the children of Diti and the sage Kasyapa. They were a race of giants who fought against the gods.

Dānavās: The Demons.

Dasaratha: King of Ayodhya and Rāma's father.

Devata: The Sanskrit word for god or deity. It can be interpreted as a demi-god, deity or any supernatural being of high eminence. Celestial being.

Devi: The female version of a Deva, i.e. a female deity or goddess. Devi is considered to be the Supreme Goddess in Saktism.

Dhāra: Flow. Reverse is Rādha, embodiment of celestial Love towards Krishna.
The spiritual heritage of India is called as Divya Dhāra, a perennial flow of divine consciousness.

Dharma: Righteous course of conduct. Can mean law, rule or duty. All eings that live in harmony with Dharma proceed quicker towards Moksha.

Dhārmic: Righteous act s that follow Dharma.

Dharmakshetra: Place where Dharma is practiced: Each person's consciousness. The Bhārata war was fought in Kurukshetra which was also called Dharmakshetra.

Dhananjaya: One of the names of Arjuna.

Dhruva: Dhruva was the son-prince of Uttānapāda. He felt humiliate d with step mother's partial attitude and left for Tapas. He and was blessed to attain eternal celestial abode as the Pole Star (Dhruva Nakshatra in Sanskrit) by Lord Vishnu. The story of Dhruva's life is often told to Hindu children as an example for perseverance, devotion, steadfastness and fearlessness. Great devotee of Lord Vishnu.

Dhritarāshtra: Father of Kauravās in Mahā Bhārata.

Durgā: A form of Devi, the supreme goddess. She is depicted as a woman riding a lion with multiple hands carrying weapons and assuming mudras. Also called Kāli.

Dwaita: A branch of Hindu philosophy, founded by Shri Madhvāchāya that advocates dualism and stresses a strict distinction between God and souls.

Dwija: A born Brahmin who does good acts. Literally it means 'twice born' i.e., first to the mother in physical form and next as an aspirant through spiritual initiation.

Fire-God: Same as Agni..

Ganapati: Remover of obstacles and the fulfiller of desire. Second son of Siva and Pārvati. Transcriber for Vyāsa, who agreed to write down without pause or hesitation the story of the Mahābhārata dictated by Vyāsa.

Ganges: A holy river in North India, believed to be a goddess by Hindus.

Ganesa: The god of good fortune, commonly identified for his elephant head.

Garuda: He is the large mythical bird or bird-like angel who appears in both Hindu and Buddhist mythology. He is the vehicle (Vāhana for Lord Vishnu.

Gāyatrī: A revered Mantra in Hinduism, found in the Yajur Veda.

Gitā: most revered scripture of Hindus found in Mahābhārata, Bhisma Parva. The great scripture of Hinduism. It stands for the Vedic principle of natural order believed to regulate and coordinate the operation of the universe on the natural, moral and sacrificial levels.

Gopa: Equivalent to a herd-boy or herd tribe

Gopāla: Name of Krishna indicating his origin as a God of flocks and herds.

Gopīkas: Gopi is a word of Sanskrit origin, meaning 'cow-herd girls'.

Guru: Revered preceptor, A spiritual teacher. In contemporary India, the title and term "Guru" is widely used within the general meaning of "wise man".

Hanumān: Monkey God, Devotee of Lord Rāma in Rāmāyana.

Hari: Hari is another name of Vishnu or God in Vaishnavism, Smārta or Adwaitan Hinduism, and appears as the 650th name in the Vishnu Sahasranāma.

Hindu Scriptures: Sacred texts of Hinduism mostly written in Sanskrit. Hindu scriptures are divided into two categories: Śruti - that which is heard (i.e. revelation) and Smriti - that which is remembered (i.e. tradition, not revelation).

Hinduism: A worldwide religious tradition based on the Vedas and Vedic scriptures. Original name is Sanātana Dharma.

Hiranyagarbha: Creative intelligence which is in a dormant stage in deluge and is also called Brahma.

Iswara: A Hindu philosophical concept of God referring to the Supreme Being which is the Lord and the ruler of everything. Hinduism uses the term Iswara exclusively to refer to the Supreme God in a monotheistic sense.

Jnamejaya: The son of Parikshiit, Grandson of Abhimanyu and great grandson of Arjuna who performed great sacrifice, Sar (Yagna).

Jnāna: Knowledge of the eternal and real.

Kailāsh: It is a peak in the Everest mountains, the source of many rivers in Asia - the Indus, the Ganges, and the Brahmaputra-and is considered as a sacred place in four religions-Hinduism, Buddhism, Jainism and Bön faith. The mountain lies near Lake Mānasarowar and Lake Rakshastal in Tibet.

Kāli: The dark, black personification of the mother-goddess, Devi whose consort is Siva.

Kali Yuga: Kali Yuga (It literally means Age of Kali). It is also known as The Age of Darkness. It is one of the four stages of development that the world goes through as part of the cycle of Yugas, as described in Hindu scriptures, the others being Dwāpara Yuga, Tretā Yuga, and Satya (Krita) Yuga.

Kalki: The tenth Avatār of Vishnu who is yet to come and appear as a 'man on horse' at the end of Kali Yuga.

Kalpa: Cycle of creation and dissolution.

Kāma: Basically it means 'desire'. The definition of Kāma also encompasses sensual gratification, sexual fulfillment, pleasure of the senses, love, and the ordinary enjoyments of life regarded as one of the four ends of man (Purushārthās).

Kārtaveerya Arjuna: Kārtavīrya Arjuna was the King of Mahishāmati, Kshatriya of Rāmāyana period believed to have a thousand arms. He had beheaded Jamadagni, father of Parasurāma. In revenge, Parasurāma killed the entire clan of Kārtavirya Arjuna. Rāvana was completely defeated and was put to humiliation by him. He is the disciple of Dattātreya.

Karma: A Sanskrit term that comprises the entire cycle of cause and effect. Work.

Karma Yoga: The practice of selfless action, Nishkāma Karma. Karma Yoga focuses on the adherence to duty (dharma) while remaining detached from the reward. It states that one can attain Moksha (salvation) by doing his duties in an unselfish manner.

Kauravās: Kaurava is a Sanskrit term, that means a descendant of Kuru dynasty,It is also the name attributed to the sons of Dhritarāshtra. It is the wicked side in Kuruksetra war with Pandavās.

Koumāra: Young adult stage, i.e., before being an adult.

Krishna: The eighth Avatār of Vishnu, one of the most worshipped Lord revered by the Hindus. Krishna is famous for his discourse to Arjuna (Bhagavad-Gita).

Krishna-Dwaipāyana: Another name of Sage Vyāsa.

Kshatriya: One of the four fundamental color castes (Varnās) in Hindu tradition, consisting of the warriors, soldiers and rulers of society.

Kshātradharma: This is a form of spiritual practice that involves "Protection of the seekers and destruction of the evildoers". In other words, it is the duty of fighting against evil as told by lord Krishna to Arjuna in the Bhagavad-Gita.

Kurma: Tortoise, The second Avatār of Vishnu in the form of a tortoise.

Kurukshetra: Place of great battle between the Pāndavās and Kauravās for the throne of Hastināpura resulted in a battle in which number of ancient kingdoms participated as allies of the rival clans. The location of the battle was Kurukshetra in the modern state of Haryāna in India.

Kurus: The name of an Indo-Aryan tribe. Their kingdom was in the Vedic civilization of India. Their kingdom was located in the area of modern Haryāna. Bhishma was their guardian.

Lakshmana: Younger step-brother of Rāma and son of Sumitra and King Dasaratha. Duryodhanā's gallant young son also bore this name.

Lakshmi: Goddess of prosperity, wealth and good fortune. She is the consort of Vishnu and an aspect of Devi.

Lankā: An island city, generally identified with Ceylon - Sri Lanka, the home of Rāvana.

Lokas: The worlds. There are supposed to be 14 worlds including the Earth.

Lord Nārāyana: Refuge of men; Vishnu. Protective aspect of Trinity.

Mādhava: One of the names of Krishna. It means the Lord of Lakshmi.

Madhusudana: Another name of Krishna, the slayer of the demon Madhu.

Mahābhārata: One of the two major ancient Sanskrit epics of India, the other being the Rāmāyana. The Mahābhārata is of religious and philosophical importance in India; which contains the Bhagavad Gita, in one of its chapters (Bhishmaparva) and a sacred text of Hinduism.

Mahādeva: Another name of Siva.

Mahā Sakti: Aspect of Feminine energy of divinity.

Mahāvishnu: Lord of the Universe who took human birth in order to wrest his kingdom from Emperor Bali for the salvation of the world. Lord Vishnu also took birth as Rāma, son of Dasaratha, to kill Rāvana, King of Lanka.

Manipuraka Chakra: 'City of jewels' in Sanskrit. Manipuraka is the third primary chakra according to Hindu tradition. It is positioned at the navel region and it has ten petals which match the Vrittis of spiritual ignorance, thirst, jealousy, treachery, shame, fear, disgust, delusion, foolishness and sadness.

Mantra: An incantation with words of power. A religious syllable or poem, typically from the Sanskrit language. They are primarily used as spiritual conduits, words and vibrations that instill one-pointed concentration in the devotee. Other purposes include religious ceremonies to accumulate wealth, avoid danger, or eliminate enemies. Mantras are performed through chanting.

Manu Smriti: The Manusmriti is the Manual of Laws of Manu. It is regarded as an important work of Hindu law and ancient Indian society. Original Manu was the forefather of all humans. There were several Manus and author of Manu Smriti is one. Some historians believe it to have been written around 200 C.E. under the reign of Pushyamitra Sunga of Sangha clan.

Mārkandeya: A sage devotee of Siva. He conquered death through devotion to the Lord Siva. He is supposed to be alive even today.

Matsya: The first Avatār of Vishnu, where he came in the form of a fish.

Māyā: Māyā is the limited, purely physical and mental reality in which our everyday consciousness has become entangled. Māyā is believed to be an illusion, a veiling power that originated from Divinity that obstructs the vision of Divinity.

Māyā Sakti: Power and energy of illusion.

Moksha: Refers to liberation from the cycle of death and rebirth. Ānanda. Bliss.

Naivedya: Food or eatables prepared as offerings to God, prior to the oblation.

Nādi: The scripture that tells about the future based on the past cycle, based on cyclical nature of cosmos. Ex: Suka Nādi, Agastya Nādi. It also means Yida, Pingala and Sushumna Nādis in the spinal column.

Nārada: Celestial sage, son of Brahma the creative aspect of trinity.

Nārasimha: The fourth Avatār of Vishnu. He is a mixed form of a man and a lion.

Nārāyana: Nārāyana is an important Sanskrit name for Vishnu. The name is also associated with Brahma and Krishna. He is also identified with, or as the son of, the original man, Purusha.

Nārāyana: Krishna's kinsmen.

Nirvāna: Literally "extinction" and/or "extinguishing", is the culmination of the yogi's pursuit of liberation. Hinduism uses the word nirvana to describe the state of Moksha, roughly equivalent to heaven. Ānanda. Bliss. Self Realization.

Nishkāma Karma: Selfless action in Karma Yoga.

OM, or Aum (ॐ): The monosyllable Mantra of high spiritual significance. The most sacred expression in Hinduism, first coming to light in the Vedic Tradition. The syllable is sometimes referred to as the **"Udgita"** or "Pranava Mantra" (Primordial Mantra); not only because it is considered to be the primal sound, but also because most Mantras begin with it.

Pāda Namaskār: Prostration at the feet with reverence and surrender.

Pancha Bhutās: The Five basic elements - earth, water, air, fire and space.

Pāndavās: Pāndavas in Sanskrit Pāndavas are the five acknowledged sons of Pāndu, by his two wives Kunti and Mādri. They are Yudhishtira, Bhima, Arjuna and Nakula, Sahadeva.

Paramātma: Soul in supreme Godhead. God.

Paramhamsa: The supreme swan. Revered sage. Self realized sage.

Parasurama: Sixth Avatāra of Vishnu, the son of Jamadagni. His name literally means Rāma-with-the-axe. He received an axe after undertaking a terrible penance to please Siva, from whom he learned the methods of warfare and other skills.

Pārtha: Another name of Arjuna.

Parikshit: Son of Abhimanyu and grandson of the Pāndavas who was crowned king after the holocaust claimed the Kauravās and the Pandavās.

Pārvatī: Goddess of love, the consort of Siva and mother of Ganesa.

Pingala: Nādi on the right side of spinal cord.

Pralaya: Deluge at the end of the world.

Pranava: Primordial vibration/sound responsible for creation to begin, OM.

Prarābdha Karma: Karmic effects experienced in this life as a result of past life actions. This cannot be escaped even by sages and saints.

Prasāda: Food or other offerings, considered to be sanctified, after being presented to God.

Purāna: Purāna means "ancient" or "old". It is the name of a genre (or a group of related genres) of Indian written literature (as distinct from oral literature). Its general themes are history, tradition and religion. These are case histories of Vedas, so that Vedic knowledge is easily understood by commoners.

Purushārthās: The four chief aims of human life. Arranged from lowest to highest, these goals are: sensual pleasures (Kāma), worldly status and security (Artha), personal righteousness and social morality (Dharma), and liberation from the cycle of reincarnation (Moksha).

Purushottama: An epithet of Sri Krishna. It is one of the names of Vishnu and means the Supreme Being.

Pushkara: The brother of Nala to whom Nala lost his kingdom and all that he possessed in gambling. Spiritual rejuvenation ceremony done for holy rivers every 12 years. It is also called Kumbha Mela in North India.

Rādhā: Rādhā is one of the Gopis (cow-herding girls) of the forest of Vrindāvan, Krishna plays with her during his upbringing as a young boy: She is the example of expansive celestial Love. In reverse it is Dhāra meaning uninterrupted flow.

Rāja Yoga: Yoga of contemplation or meditation, includes Patanjali Ashtānga Yoga. Also called Dhyāna Yoga.

Rākshasa: A Rākshasa alternately, Rākshas is a demon or unrighteous spirit in Hinduism.

Rāma: The Seventh Avatāra of Vishnu. The life and heroic deeds of Rāma are written in the Sanskrit epic, The Rāmāyana.

Rāmānuja: Saint philosopher who propagated Visishtādwaita (qualified non-dualism (1017-1137).

Rāmāyana: The great Indian Epic. Part of the Hindu Smriti, written by Vālmiki. This epic of 24,000 verses in seven Kāndās (chapters or books) tells of a Raghuvamsa prince, Rāma of Ayodhya, whose wife Sita was abducted by the demon king Rāvana.

Rāvana: King of Lanka who abducted Sita, the beautiful wife of Rāmachandra. Rāvana is depicted in art with ten heads, signifying that he had knowledge spanning all the ten directions.

Rig-Veda: The Rig-Veda is a collection of Vedic Sanskrit hymns counted as the holiest of the four religious texts of Hindus, known as the Vedas.

Rishi: Rishi, also known as Mantradrashta ("Seer of the Mantras") and Vedavaktāra ("chanter of the Vedas") is a seer who "heard" (cf. Sruti) the hymns of the Vedās. A Rishi is regarded as a combination of a patriarch, a priest, a preceptor, an author of Vedic hymns, a sage, a saint, an ascetic, a prophet and a hermit into one.

Rudra: A Rig Vedic God of the storm, the hunt, death, Nature and the Wind. Rudra is an early form of Siva and a name of Siva in the Siva Sahasranāma.

Sādhana: Spiritual practice/exercise by a Sādhu or a Sādhaka (practitioner) to attain Moksha, which is liberation from the cycle of birth and death (Samsāra), or a particular goal such as blessing from a deity.

Samādhi: A term used in yogic meditation. Samādhi is also the Hindi word for a structure commemorating the dead. Sepulcher.

Sāmkhya: A school of philosophy emphasizing a dualism between Purusha and Prakrti, propounded by sage Kapila.

Samsāra: Means world of ups and downs. The world of contemporary reality (Māya or illusion).

Samatvam: Equal mindedness; equanimity, balance.

Samudra Manthan: Samudra Manthan or The churning of the ocean of milk is one of the most famous episodes in the Puranas and is celebrated in a major way every twelve years in the festival known as Kumbha Mela. It is also called Ksheerasāgar Madhanam. Demi-Gods and Demons churn the milky ocean for obtaining Amrit (celestial nectar).

Sangham: Society we live in.

Sanchita Karma: Kārmic baggage that will produce results in future lives.

Sanyāsin: One who has renounced the world and its concerns.

Saraswati: Saraswati is the first of the three great goddesses of Hinduism, the other two being Lakshmi and Durga. Saraswati is the consort of Lord Brahmā, the Creator. It is river above Sindhu that dried out.

Sat Guru: An evolved spiritual preceptor.

Satya Nārāyana: Vishnu, Embodiment as Krishna.

Sakti: An aspect of Devi and a personification of God as the Divine Mother who represents the active, dynamic principles of feminine power.

Saktism: Sākteyam Lit., "doctrine of power" or "doctrine of the Goddess") is a denomination of Hinduism that focuses worship upon Sakti or Devi – the Hindu Divine Mother – as the absolute, ultimate Godhead. It is, along with Saivism and Vaisnavism, one of the three primary schools of Hinduism.

Sankara: A name of Siva; Also the name of Sankarāchārya, the proponent of non-dualism (Adwaita).

Satrughna: One of Dasharathā's four sons, King of Madhu.

Śatapatha Brāhmana: Satapatha Brāhmana ("Brāhmana of one-hundred paths" - abbreviated ŚB) is one of the prose texts describing the Vedic ritual, associated with the White Yajurveda.

Saivism: Saivism names the oldest of the four sects of Hinduism. Followers of Saivism, called "Saivās", and also "Saivates", revere Siva as the Supreme Being.

Siva: A form of Isvara or God in Saivism. Śiva is commonly known as "the destroyer" and is the third god of the Trimurti (Trinity).

Sri: Another name of Lakshmi, a goddess, the delight of Vishnu.

Sri Krishna: One of the ten Avatārs of Lord Vishnu, narrator of Bhagavad-Gita.

Sudra: One of the four castes in Hindu tradition, consisting of artisans, cleaners and laborers.

Sindhu: The Indus River, It is the longest and most important river in Pakistan. Originating in the Tibetan plateau in the vicinity of Lake Mānsarovar. The name Hindu was derived from Sindhu.

Sītā: Sita was the wife of Rāma, and is esteemed an exemplar of womanly and wifely virtue. Sita was herself an Avatāra of Lakshmi, Vishnu's eternal consort, who chose to reincarnate herself on Earth as Sita, and endure an arduous life, in order to provide humankind an example of such virtues.

Sloka: A verse of lines in Sanskrit, typically recited as a prayer.

Smriti: Memorized and reproduced knowledge.

Sri Rāma: Also known as Rāma, Rāmachandra or Sri Rāma. This king of Ayodhya was banished to the forest for fourteen years, killed Rāvana the king of Lanka who abducted his wife, Sita. Avatār of Vishnu.

Śruti: A canon of Hindu scriptures. Sruti is believed to have no author; rather a divine recording of the "cosmic sounds of truth", Revelations, heard by Rishis.

Sthitaprajna: person with equanimity; equal minded person: self realized person.

Śuka: A sage, son of Veda Vyāsa, who related the Bhāgavata Purāna to King Parikshit, son of Abhimanyu, grandson of Arjuna.

Sūrya: A solar deity who is one of the three main Vedic Gods.

Susruta Samhita: Suśruta Samhita is a Sanskrit redaction text on all of the major concepts of Āyurvedic medicine with innovative chapters on surgery, attributed to Susruta, likely a historical sage physician of 6th century BC.

Sushamna Nādi: The Nādi in the middle of Yida and Pingala that channels spiritual energy upwards with spiritual practice.

Sūtra: Sūtra refers to an aphorism or a collection of such aphorisms in the form of a book or text. 'Sutrās' form a school of Vedic study, related to and somewhat later than the Upanishads.

Swami Vivekananda: The Indian monk. Disciple of Ramakrishna, who propagated Hinduism to the West.

Sudra: The one who belonged to the lower caste of Hinduism. Blue collar worker. Manual labor.

Svarupam: True nature of a person.

Swarga: The Paradise, a place where all wishes and desires are gratified, The heaven of Indra where mortals after death enjoy the results of their good deeds on earth.

Tantra: The esoteric Hindu traditions of rituals and yoga. Tantra can be summarized as a family of voluntary rituals modeled on those of the Vedas, together with their attendant texts and lineages.

Trikarana Suddhi: Unison of thoughts, words and deeds. Purity of heart.

Tulasi Dās: Goswāmi Tulsidās (1532–1623) was a Hindu poet and philosopher, translator of the epics into vernacular. Tulsidas wrote twelve books and is considered the greatest and most famous of Hindi poets.

Upanishad: Part of the Hindu Śruti scriptures which primarily discuss meditation and philosophy, seen as religious instructions by most schools of Hinduism.

Uttar kānda: The end-part of epic Rāmāyana added later to the work of Valmiki.

Varāha: The third Avatār of the Hindu Godhead Vishnu, in the form of a Boar. He appeared in order to defeat Hiranyāksha, a demon who had taken the Earth (Prithvi) and carried it to the bottom of what is described as the cosmic ocean in the story.

Vaiśampāyana: A celebrated sage who was the original teacher of the Black (Krishna) Yajur-Veda. He was a pupil of the great Vyāsa, from whom he learned the Mahābhārata, which he afterwards recited to King Janamejaya at a festival.

Vaishnavism: Vaishnavism is a tradition of Hinduism, distinguished from other schools by its worship of Vishnu or his associated Avatārs, principally as Rāma and Krishna, as the original and supreme Gods.

Vaisya: One of the four fundamental Varnās (colors) in Hindu caste tradition comprising merchants, artisans, and landowners.

Vālmikī: Mahārishi Vālmiki is the author of the Hindu epic Rāmāyana, connected with the kings of Ayodhya, contemporary of Rāma who invented the Sloka meter and who taught the Rāmāyana to Kusa and Lava, the sons of Rāma.

Vānaprastha: The third stage of the Dwijā's life, when he is required to relinquish worldly responsibilities to his heirs and retire to the woods with his wife for an anchorite's life. A person who is living in the forest as a hermit after giving up material desires.

Varāha: The third Avatār of Vishnu, who came in the form of a boar.

Varna: Means - color, Varna refers to the four naturally existing classes of society as given in the Hindu scriptures: Brāhmin, Kshatriya, Vaisha and Sudra.

Varuna: A god of the sky, of rain and of the celestial ocean, as well as a god of law and of the underworld.

Vasishta: Vasishta was chief of the seven venerated sages (or Saptarishis) and the Rājaguru of the Suryavamsa. He was the Mānasaputra of Brahma. He had in his possession the divine cow Kāmadhenu, and Nandini, her child, who could grant anything to their owners. Arundhati was his wife.

Vāyu: The god of air and wind who is also father of Bhima and Hanumān.

Veda: Collectively refers to a corpus of ancient Indo-Aryan religious literature that is considered by adherents of Hinduism to be revealed knowledge. Many Hindus believe that the Vedas existed since the beginning of creation.

Vedānta: Philosophy based on Vedas, Upanishads. Highest philosophy.

Veda Vyāsa: Vyāsa, author of the Mahābhārata.

Vipra: A Brahmin who is well versed in Vedās.

Vishada: Sorrow caused by life. Grief.

Vishnu: A form of God, to whom many Hindus pray. For Vaishnavas, He is the only Ultimate Reality or God. In Trimurty (Trinity), He is the second aspect of God in the Trimurti (also called the Hindu Trinity), along with Brahma and Siva. Known as the Preserver, He is most famously identified with His Avatārs, especially Krishna and Rāma.

Visishtādwaita: Philosophy based on qualified non-dualism, propagated by the saint Rāmānuja (1017-1137).

Viswarupa: All-pervading, all-including form. See the description in the Bhagavad-Gita chapter eleven.

Vivekananda: Disciple of Ramakrishna who propagated Hinduism to west.

Vrindāvana: A wood in the district of Mathura where Krishna passed his youth, under the name of Gopāla, among the cowherds.

Vyāsa: Compiler of the Vedas, son of sage Parāsara.

Yādavās: The descendants of Yadu, who dwelt by the Yamuna river.

Yajna: A Vedic ritual of sacrifice performed to please the Devās, or sometimes to the Supreme Spirit Brahman. Often it involves a fire, which represents the god Agni, in the centre of the stage and items are offered into the fire.

Yama: A Yama (Sanskrit), literally translates as a "restraint", a rule or code of conduct for living virtuously.

Yavvana: Youth stage of life.

Yoga: Spiritual practices performed primarily as a means to enlightenment (or Bodhi). Traditionally, Karma Yoga, Bhakti Yoga, Jnāna Yoga, and Rāja Yoga are considered the four main Yogās. In the West, Yoga has become mainly associated with the Āsanas (postures) of Hatha Yoga, popular as fitness exercises.

Yoga Sutra: One of the six Darsanās of Hindu or Vedic schools and, alongside the Bhagavad-Gita and Hatha Yoga Pradipika, Patanjali Ashtānga Yoga are the milestone in the history of Yoga.

Yogi: One who practices yoga. These designations are mostly reserved for advanced practitioners. The word "Yoga" itself—from the Sanskrit root Yuj ("to yoke") --is generally translated as "union" or "integration" and may be understood as union with the Divine, or integration of body, mind, and spirit.

Yida: Nadi that is on the left side of spinal cord.

Yuga: In Hindu philosophy (and in the teachings of Surat Sabda Yoga) the cycle of creation is divided into four Yugas (ages or eras).

Yuga Dharma: One aspect of Dharma, as understood by Hindus. Yuga Dharma is an aspect of dharma that is valid for a Yuga. The other aspect of Dharma is Sanātana Dharma, dharma which is valid for eternity.

EPILOGUE

Exploring Hinduism in depth is exploring life and living. It has been a wonderful and enjoyable journey. The more I pierce through the deeper layers of understanding, the more I have realized the truth in the words of Swami Vivekananda:

"If there were to be a single universal religion in the world, that would be Vedāntic Hinduism".

Hinduism is one religion that promotes full expansion of human potential. Through this full expansion, the petty boundaries and divisions of caste, creed, race, religion and nationalities that encompassed and enslaved mankind across the globe fall apart. Humanity appears as one universal family (Vasudhaika Kutumbakam). It is all inclusive of the entire humanity, making the world a heaven of universal harmony. It brings this harmony inside out. I thoroughly enjoyed putting my deeper experiences into this book and I sincerely hope that the reader will get as much joy reading it.

LOKĀN SAMASTĀ SUKHINO BHAVANTU
(May all the beings in all the worlds be happy)